Into the Dark

Into The Dark

A Bomber Command Story of
Combat and Survival, Discovery
and Remembrance

**Janet Hughes
(née Wilson) and
Reginald Wilson**

Published in 2015 by Fighting High Ltd,
www.fightinghigh.com

British Library Cataloguing-in-Publication data.
A CIP record for this title is available from the
British Library.

ISBN – 13: 978-0992620769

Designed and typeset in Adobe Minion 11/15pt
by Michael Lindley, www.truthstudio.co.uk.

Printed and bound in China by Toppan Leefung.
Front cover design by www.truthstudio.co.uk.

Dedication

To all who served as aircrew in Bomber Command, and in particular to the 55,573 who 'failed to return', of whom many were never found or definitively identified. This book is dedicated to their memory.

Contents

Prologue

Berlin, Thursday, 16 October 2008

'Beneath the gentle autumn sun …' intoned the television presenter, as he described the deeply moving scene that was unfolding before him. Barbara Wilson, then seventy-eight years old, turned to me, her elder daughter Janet, and with her eyes full of wonder and glistening with emotion, softly breathed these words: 'Just think, your father started all this!'

Reginald Wilson is a veteran of Bomber Command, and served with 102 Squadron of the RAF during the Second World War. In recent years, his incredible tenacity has led to an amazing discovery, which no one could have anticipated or predicted. Each time Reg's story is told, listeners agree that it is truly astonishing. If someone were to write a fictional account telling a similar story, it would never be taken seriously, as it would be considered too far-fetched to be credible.

> '*Strange – but true; for truth is always strange;*
> *Stranger than fiction.*'

Lord Byron wrote these words in 1823. Reg Wilson was born one hundred years later, in 1923. Much can be learned from his true, if incredible, story. Not least, it reminds us of the way in which so many brave young men rose to the challenge in our country's hour of need. They went away as overgrown schoolboys, and came back – if they were lucky enough to do so – as inured men, permanently altered by their harrowing experiences. My paternal grandmother once commented that Reg had never been the same after he returned from the war. She never really explained what she meant by this, but I now believe that Reg's inclination to be overcautious, his inability to let go, to take risks and to have fun, and his tendency to see the glass as always being half empty, rather than half full, was the result of never having come to terms with his traumatic experiences.

These days, nothing ever arouses such passion in Reg as talking about the cause for which he fought. As a young man, full of missionary zeal, he believed so fervently in freedom, justice and democracy. With the passion and idealism that one only finds in the young, he was prepared to lay down his life for these principles. Even now, at ninety-two, he never wavers from his belief that he did the right thing for the right reasons.

However, perhaps the most important legacy of Reg's story is that it illustrates the spirit of reconciliation that now exists between nations which were at war with each other some seventy years ago. It tells of friendships resulting from the state of total war that once divided our countries. It is a story of closure with the past and of hope for the future.

Janet Hughes (née Wilson), 31 January 2015.

Part One
Training and
Operations

W. Roche
GOODMAYES

(*Images on previous pages*)
Royal Air Force navigator Reg
Wilson. Late 1942 /early 1943.

St Paul's Cathedral stands
defiant amid the onslaught of
the Luftwaffe on 29 December
1940, like the phoenix arising
from the ashes. (*Daily Mail*)

Chapter 1

The Calling

'But when I look round to see how we can win the war I see that there is only one sure path. We have no Continental army which can defeat the German military power. The blockade is broken and Hitler has Asia and probably Africa to draw from. Should he be repulsed here or not try invasion he will recoil eastward, and we have nothing to stop him. But there is one thing that will bring him back and bring him down, and that is an absolutely devastating, exterminating attack by very heavy bombers from this country upon the Nazi homeland. We must be able to overwhelm them by this means, without which I do not see a way through.'

Winston Churchill to Lord Beaverbrook (Minister of Aircraft Production), Minute of 8 July 1940 about Bomber Command – made after the fall of France and the retreat of the British forces from Dunkirk, when Britain stood alone against the might of Germany under the control of Hitler.

Strong words, but, in my opinion, justified by the following circumstances.

On the morning of 30 December 1940, I struggled into London to my workplace at Blackfriars. Transport was disrupted to the point where I had had to abandon my efforts to travel in by public transport from my home in Goodmayes, near Ilford, Essex. The devastation in the City of London was catastrophic, even by the standards of that terrible year of the Blitz. The twelve-hour night bombing raid of 29/30 December, and the subsequent fire storm, had destroyed a huge area, stretching from Islington to the edge of St Paul's churchyard. I later learned that it had been timed to coincide with a particularly low tide on the River Thames, thereby making water difficult to obtain for firefighting. When I arrived in the City that morning, in my city, I was heartbroken to see the destruction around me. I stood in horror as I looked up Ludgate Hill to St Paul's Cathedral, silhouetted against the smoke and the still-smouldering buildings, just as in the (now famous) photograph that would appear in the next day's edition of the *Daily Mail*.

Enough was enough. I surveyed the scene before me and made my decision. I had to do something. I resolved to join the RAF as a volunteer. Although I was not quite eighteen years old, I wanted to train as a fighter pilot, and do battle against the Nazi war machine, not just to save my beloved country, but also to keep the torch of freedom burning for Britain and for occupied Europe.

The night of 29/30 December was the last straw as far as I was concerned. In all, before I eventually joined up as aircrew in August 1941, I experienced seventy-eight consecutive nights when the German bombers flew up the Thames and attacked London. East London experienced extensive damage and suffered many thousands of civilian casualties.

On 29 December 1943, exactly three years later to the night, to quote Churchill once more, I 'gave it to them back!' I flew as a navigator in a Halifax aircraft, as one of a force of over 700 bombers, to Berlin. It was the fifth heaviest raid ever made against Berlin, and over 2,300 tons of incendiaries and bombs were dropped in about twenty minutes.

I joined the RAF Volunteer Reserve (RAFVR) in August 1941. I wore a white flash in my forage cap to indicate that I was a member of aircrew, and after a long wait at St John's Wood, London, I was posted to the Initial Training Wing, Torquay, Devon.

Here I learned the rudiments of subjects such as meteorology, air navigation, aircraft recognition, wireless telegraphy, etc, alongside some square bashing and clay pigeon shooting. I was promoted from AC2 to LAC and posted to Marshalls airfield, Cambridge, for a flying test. I flew with an instructor in a Tiger Moth for about eight hours and passed the initial experience requirement necessary to join the Arnold Training Scheme in the USA.

After some Christmas leave and a short stay at Heaton Park, Manchester,

I joined the troopship *Montcalm* at Gourock, on the Clyde, bound for Halifax, Canada. It is prophetic, in view of later developments, that we were heading for a place called Halifax! We were accompanied by another troop ship, the *Vollendam*, and we were supposed to have had a destroyer as an escort for the crossing. Unfortunately, the destroyer had to return to base. (It was a First World War American destroyer, one of fifty given to Britain in exchange for the use of Bermuda, I believe, and it could not cope with the bad weather we were experiencing.)

Luckily, our two-week crossing in January 1942 was uneventful, although half a dozen ships, which were in the same area of the Atlantic at that time, were sunk. At that point in the war, as many as sixty ships a week were destroyed by German U-boats in the North Atlantic.

From Halifax we were the first RAF aircrew trainees to travel to the USA in uniform. America had become our ally just a few weeks beforehand. This was after the infamy of the Japanese bombing of Pearl Harbor on 7 December 1941, an event that had happened without any formal declaration of war, and much of the Pacific fleet was sunk in the process. We had suffered many privations in Britain – bombing, blackout, blockade, the rationing of virtually everything, and military setbacks such as the fall of Norway and of France and the problems in the Middle East – so America was for us, without any doubt, the land of milk and honey!

We travelled to 'Turner Field' in Albany, Georgia, for a month's acclimatisation, during which time I celebrated my nineteenth birthday. Turner Field was a base for the American Army Air Corps cadets. Here we were given Army Air Corps clothing, and we were to be treated like the cadets. In practice, this meant:

- Drilling and physical training (callisthenics at six o'clock in the morning!).
- Being given literature on expected behaviour and etiquette.
- Marching behind a brass band, playing Army Air Corps music, prior to all meals and also before Retreat (the lowering of the American flag in the evening).

Having endured basic rations in Britain for a considerable time, every meal at Turner Field was a feast and, as cadets, we were waited on hand and foot by coloured waiters (at this time, in the South, coloured people were not considered equal to whites; they were required to sit in the back of buses and in separate parts of the cinema etc, and were treated generally as second-class citizens). Back in Britain you had to queue up for your meals, get all your meal on one plate, take your own cutlery (in your gasmask case) and wash it up afterwards in a tank of tepid greasy water!

After a month, in March 1942 I was posted to Lakeland, Florida, to a civilian flying school for Primary Flying Training. Here I had a very pleasant time indeed. I went solo in a Stearman biplane, after the instructor had 'buzzed off' a herd of cows from the auxiliary landing field by diving at them! I completed forty hours of solo flying, much of which included aerobatics – stalls, spins, loops, etc. The flying was over lakes and orange groves in the Florida sunshine. As English cadets, we enjoyed much hospitality with local American families and their daughters!

After completion of the course, we had a few days' leave, and a colleague and I hitched a lift to West Palm Beach. We booked into a hotel, but within a short while we were invited to stay with an American lady (Mrs Hubbard), who turned out to be the daughter of Rockefeller (a multimillionaire and philanthropist). She had an English woman staying with her, who had a son in the RAF, and the two ladies looked after us for the next couple of days as if we were two long lost sons! Mrs Hubbard's house could have been in Hollywood: it had a beautiful swimming pool within a magnificent Italian-styled garden, with an arcaded drinks bar at one end.

My most powerful memory of this time was to meet – and be photographed with – one of the few surviving Fleet Air Arm pilots, who in the previous year had torpedoed the pocket battleship *Bismarck*, damaged its rudder, and enabled the British Fleet to sink it in the Atlantic Ocean. He was touring America as a hero, and had been invited to Mrs Hubbard's home. (The sinking of the *Bismarck* was a great British victory, as it had previously attacked and sunk one of our battleships *Hood*, with the loss of nearly 1,500 lives.)

After this short break, at the end of April 1942 we were posted to an Army Air Corps flying school in Georgia for Intermediate Training. Here

I started a course of flying on a basic trainer with an Army instructor. After a number of flying lessons, I was unable to convince my instructor that I was safe to go solo on this plane, and that was the end of my pilot training. (The US Army Air Corps had a policy of failing a high proportion of cadets, and I was one of them; had I been trained in an RAF flying school in the States, the story might have been different.) I was disheartened at the time, but took the somewhat philosophical view that I could have been killed myself out there in Georgia, as one of my friends was, on a simple training exercise that went wrong. At least, if I died in combat, it would be for a just cause.

In June 1942, I took the train back to Canada to the Royal Canadian Air Force (RCAF) camp at Trenton, Ontario, and after some interviews and an exam, I remustered to U/T navigator. This transfer gave me an unexpected chance to see some more of Canada, and I was able to visit Lake Ontario, Toronto and Niagara Falls before I moved on.

A party of us was then moved westwards on a journey that took us by train through impressive Canadian countryside, with pine forests, and rivers solid with floating logs. The train was pulled by an enormous steam engine, snorting its way through this majestic scenery with hardly a sign of civilisation anywhere. We stopped eventually at Brandon, Manitoba, where we stayed awaiting a posting to an air navigation school. While at Brandon, I managed to spend a weekend at Clear Lake, about 60 miles north. It was a beautiful lake surrounded by pine forests, with log cabins, a restaurant, and a central hall. Swimming, fishing and rowing facilities were available. In the evening, dances were held in the hall and a Royal Canadian Mounted Policeman was in attendance – it was just like a picture postcard! At a dance there, I met a girl who lived in Winnipeg, and whom I was able to see again on a number of occasions as I was posted to the Winnipeg Air Navigation School about a week later (August 1942). The school services were run by civilians, with the teaching of all the subjects being carried out by the RCAF. Winnipeg is situated in the vast grain-growing area of Manitoba, which is as flat as a pancake. When flying at a few thousand feet, you have an unrestricted view as far as the horizon. The towns, marked by grain elevators and water towers (with the town's name painted on the side), were spaced along the railway line, with other settlements scattered in the countryside. All of these were visible from any cross-country route, thus it was impossible to get lost during navigational exercises, even at night as there was no blackout in Canada.

It was a pleasant, comfortable three months' training, spending about half our time in the classroom, and half on air exercises. We flew in ancient Anson aircraft, with civilian pilots, and in addition to our air exercises, we had to manually wind up the wheels on take-off and down again on landing.

The main things I can remember from this time are the crash of a light aircraft only a few yards away from us, and the raging fire that ensued, which made it impossible to rescue the pilot, and the freezing nights practising astro sextant shots. I also recall the more pleasant activity of eating Christmas-like turkey dinners every Sunday, and going to dances in Winnipeg at weekends with my female friend, whom I had met at Clear Lake, Brandon.

I was awarded my Navigator's Wing on 20 November 1942, and was promoted to the rank of Flight Sergeant. I was just a few marks short of getting a commission.

A few days later, we were all on the long train journey back to Moncton, Halifax, breaking our trip for a memorable stopover in Montreal. We returned to England on the luxury liner, Queen Elizabeth, which had been converted into a troopship. We had two meals a day, there were seventeen bunks to a state cabin, and we travelled without escort, taking only four days to cross the North Atlantic. We were home on leave for Christmas. Just one year had elapsed since I was on embarkation leave for my training in North America.

Chapter 2

Training for War

The beginning of 1943 brought about a glut of trained aircrew from the North American and Commonwealth training schools. As a result, many hundreds of us were held in holding centres in Harrogate and Bournemouth, to await postings. To fill in the time, I was transferred with others to an RAF Regiment Training Course at Whitley Bay, on the coast near Newcastle, in the freezing weather of February 1943.

It was not until late April 1943 that we took up flying again, when a party of us was posted to the RAF Air Navigation School at Jurby, at the northern end of the Isle of Man. For the next three weeks, still flying in Ansons, I brushed up my navigation skills (not having flown for five months) with day and night cross-country exercises around the Irish Sea, the east coast of Northern Ireland and the west coast of Britain. The weather was quite cold for the time of year, and we even experienced snow in the first two weeks of May. On free days, we would take the small 'toast rack' railway from Jurby to Douglas (capital of the Isle of Man) for a day out – it was very quiet in wartime. My abiding memory of this period is seeing all the hotels along the sea front, which were wired off, as they housed many of the 'aliens' who had been interned there for the duration of the war.

On the completion of the course we were granted some leave, and then I was posted to the RAF Operational Training Unit at Kinloss, Scotland, on the Moray Firth. I was now set for 'crewing up' in Bomber Command and getting nearer to operational flying.

I arrived at Kinloss in the first week in June. The weather was marvellous and stayed like it for the six weeks that we were there. For part of the time, a party of us were housed in a large mansion-like property (just for sleeping purposes) and each of us was given a bike to get to and from the airfield. The countryside was beautiful and with the consistent fine weather and the birds singing in the trees and hedgerows, cycling was an added pleasure. It was so peaceful. The war seemed very far away indeed.

RAF Kinloss was equipped with Whitley bombers (withdrawn from operational flying in 1942) and these were known as 'flying coffins' as they were very sluggish in responding to the flying controls. This was a major defect, as we were to discover when flying in formation over Elgin to celebrate a special occasion.

After a few days, we were crewed up, and our crew consisted of:

F/O S.R. Vivian	Pilot	'Viv'
F/Sgt R.C. Wilson	Navigator	'Reg'
F/O L.A. Underwood	Bomb aimer	'Laurie'
Sgt W. Ross	W/OP, AG	'Bill'
Sgt J. Bushell	Rear AG	'John'

During the ensuing six weeks, we had frequent day and night flying, carrying out exercises such as cross-country and formation flying, air firing, fighter affiliation and bombing practice. We also had to undertake some ground work. I can remember being introduced to the Distant Reading Compass, located near the tail of the aircraft, away from magnetic influences. It was a giro-controlled compass, and was very stable (it could be adjusted by the navigator for the earth's magnetic variation to give true north readings), and had electric repeaters for the pilot, navigator and bomb aimer. I can also remember flying at night, trying to practise astro-navigation, with the sky being barely dark! In the north of Scotland in midsummer at a height of 10,000 feet, the sun's glow was present on the horizon for most of the night. In this light, the Grampians and the Highlands below looked gaunt and forbidding.

By the end of our training, our crew had become great friends. We spent time together at Findhorn Bay (on the Moray Firth) on some afternoons, and in the pub in Forres town on some Saturdays. We spent one entire weekend in the mess, having been confined to the station by the CO because we had landed in error at RAF Lossiemouth (an adjacent airfield on the Moray Firth) instead of Kinloss. We drank a lot of beer that weekend!

We left Kinloss for some leave towards the end of July, never to see 'Viv', our pilot, again. Little did we know that he would be killed three weeks later (just a few days after getting married while on leave). This was before we even reached RAF Rufforth in Yorkshire, our Conversion Unit for Halifax heavy bombers. We arrived at RAF Rufforth in the middle of August to find that 'Viv' had been reported missing on 10 August 1943, while flying as second pilot on a raid to Nuremberg. (I have learned since that his aircraft crashed near Ramsen/Bolanden, Germany. Six were killed, including 'Viv' and two became POWs). All pilots, as captains of their aircraft, had to have experienced two operational flights – 'second dickey' trips – before they could fly their own crews on operations. 'Viv' was on the second of these flights, and so never got to head his own crew on an operation. We were therefore a headless crew, awaiting the appointment of another pilot.

From then on, it would be apparent that our lives in Bomber Command were becoming a lottery. There was no way we could tell from day to day, even at a Conversion Unit before operations started, whether we would die, or live to see another day. During our short stay at Rufforth, about sixty aircrew were killed due to mechanical failure or accidents. Among other incidents, I can remember the collision of two aircraft in mid-air, and that another aircraft crashed when its propeller flew off into the fuselage. A further aircraft came down at night on a practice bombing raid exercise.

After a few days, F/Lt P.G.A. Harvey was appointed as our pilot, and Sgt A. McCarroll as our mid-upper gunner. The latter had formerly been the drummer in Maurice Winnick's dance band, and was well known on BBC radio in the pre-war period. Sgt J. McArdle was to be our flight engineer. This completed the crew for our four-engined bomber, the Halifax.

F/Lt Harvey was an experienced pilot, having survived two operational tours in the Middle East in 1941 on Wellington bombers. It was a mystery to us why he was taking on another tour. However, flying on operations deep inside Germany in 1943 was another dimension for him, as cities in Germany were heavily defended by ack-ack, and night fighters were armed with cannon and equipped with radar homing devices. This was a very different scenario to his experiences in the Middle East in 1941, especially in view of the fact that many of his sorties, although being in a war zone, had not been bombing missions.

As F/Lt Harvey was a seasoned pilot, the minimum time was taken to crew up, get familiar with the Halifax, and take on the new disciplines of a flight engineer and a mid-upper gunner. For my part, I had to learn how to use 'Gee'. This was a radar device for measuring pulses from two transmitting stations displayed on a cathode ray tube, which were then plotted on a special gridded map, to give pinpoint accuracy of one's ground position.

There were air exercises for bombing, air firing and fighter affiliation. The latter exercise was one to remember. The date was 2 September 1943. For this exercise, we flew at 10,000 feet and a fighter would 'attack' from behind. The two gunners would then cooperate with the pilot so that he could take evasive action. F/Lt Harvey, in taking evasive action, managed to turn the aircraft on its back, and it was several thousand feet later before he succeeded in righting the aircraft again. I had spun round in the nose of the plane, broken rivets were rattling around inside the fuselage, and the chemical Elsan toilet at the back of the aircraft had emptied its contents all over the rear of the plane!

We were all shaken up by the experience, especially as F/Lt Harvey already had 390 operational flying hours to his credit, and we did not expect him to lose control. However, some good came out of it, in that John, the rear gunner, decided that from then on he would store his parachute in his gun turret, rather than in the fuselage as required by regulations. This action would later save his life.

I also resolved that I would be prepared for the worst and have a routine to cover baling out. I devised the following procedure:

'Helmet off'   (You could break your neck with the
                                          helmet still attached to the oxygen
                                          supply and intercom.)

'Parachute on'   (Not a good idea to jump out
                                          without it!)

'Handle on the left-hand side'   I am left handed. (Aircrew were
                                 sometimes killed due to an unopened
                                 parachute with the handle – D ring –
                                 on the 'wrong' side.)

In addition, I decided that, as navigator, I had a minute or so to spare
while over the target, so I could fold back my seat, lift up the navigation
table clear of the escape hatch and be ready to bale out immediately if
necessary. I believe that these plans, together with the action taken by
John, the rear gunner, gave me and Laurie (the bomb aimer) additional
vital seconds, when the three of us were to save our lives nearly five
months later.

In a week or so we were posted to 102 Squadron to commence our
operational service.

Pocklington airfield was situated 12 miles south-east of York, with 800-
foot hills 3½ miles north-east of the airfield. While I was there, two Halifax
bombers with heavy bombloads crashed into these hills after take-off –
that particular runway was not used subsequently. Pocklington was just
a wartime airfield, with only temporary accommodation; thus all our
billets were in Nissen huts. They had semicircular corrugated-iron
roofs and walls, with concrete ends. They were dispersed in fields near
the airfield and were dreary, inhospitable places in winter, each heated
only by a small central coal-burning stove. Consequently, whenever possible, when not on duty, we sought refuge and relaxation in the relative
comfort of the sergeants' mess, or in the pubs, such as Betty's Bar, or in
the dance halls, like De Grey Rooms in the city of York.

Pocklington had three affiliated airfields: Elvington, Full Sutton and
Melbourne. All the airfields were commanded by Air Commodore
'Gus' Walker, who was at that time the youngest air commodore in the
RAF, aged just thirty-one. He had lost his right arm when a Lancaster
exploded on the ground at Syerston, the airfield which he commanded,
in 1942.

We arrived at Pocklington in mid-September 1943. F/Lt Harvey was
promoted to Acting Squadron Leader in charge of 'A' Flight, and we became
his crew, which meant we would not fly as frequently on operations as

other crews. (This was considered to be a mixed blessing, as a tour –
thirty operations – would take longer under his command.)

Over the next two weeks we completed a number of cross-country
exercises, mostly for me to practise my navigation skills with new
equipment. At Rufforth I had mastered Gee radar, which enabled me to
plot accurate ground positions essential for calculating wind velocities
– the basis of all air navigation. Unfortunately, the Germans had learned
how to jam this equipment, so that as an aircraft approached the coast-
line of continental Europe, the radar pulses were obliterated. This meant
that the navigator had a race against time to obtain as much data as he
could in the short time available.

At Pocklington we had a very new piece of radar equipment called 'H2S'
(height to surface). Located in the aircraft itself, it sent out pulses to the
ground around the aircraft for 15–20 miles. Reflections were received back
as bright specks on a cathode ray tube. The density of the reflections
depended on whether the aircraft was flying over sea, land, hills, rivers,
cities or lakes. The reflections were then translated into a rough topographical map of the ground, although the quality of the picture varied
from time to time. The map was displayed on the cathode ray screen.

The best map results were produced between land and sea, but provided
that the navigator was reasonably aware of his ground position, he could
recognise coastlines, large rivers and lakes, and sizeable towns, both on
the way to and returning from a target. With this, the navigator could
accurately plot the bearing and distance from these landmarks, and so
be able to recalculate wind velocities, required tracks, ground speeds and
the time required to reach the target. With the help of H2S, some more-
experienced navigators would have the ability to blind bomb, without the
need to use the markers dropped by the Pathfinders (who incidentally
also used H2S equipment). H2S could not be jammed, but night fighters
could 'home in' on the H2S frequency if it was continuously switched
on. This hazard was not known to aircrews for some time after the system
was in operation, and some aircraft were shot down because of it.

Another new piece of equipment, called the 'air plot indicator' was
also available to the navigator by this time. This linked the giro compass
and airspeed indicator to provide a continuous read-out of the air
position in latitude and longitude. It was a useful guide to have available,

but no navigator would rely on it entirely. He would always consult his own air plot, as drawn on his own navigational chart.

We also had a hand-held 'ICAN computer'. This was a manually operated vectoring device, on which we could plot a course and calculate the airspeed, to make good our desired track and ground speed, before we added this information to our main chart. Two other navigational aids we had used in training were radio bearings, taken by the wireless operator, and our own astro sight shots. The astro shots were converted to position lines by use of air almanacs. However, neither of these methods was practical when operating over enemy territory. This was because operational aircraft were growing faster, so the potential need to take evasive action at any moment (because of flak or night fighters) would make these methods inoperable.

There were times when no navigational aids were available to us at all, and map-reading over cloud or at night, especially at high altitude, was not possible. At these times, we had to resort to 'dead reckoning' methods. These methods required accurate plotting of the air position and the use of wind velocities, which were supplied by the meteorology officer, or the use of those already calculated by the navigator en route. In both these cases, they would need to be modified to cater for changes to the forecast weather, and to take account of wind velocity changes and any alterations in altitude that became necessary during the flight.

Preparing for a bombing mission on an operational squadron was quite a lengthy procedure, occupying a good part of the day prior to the night's operation. About mid-morning 'Ops On' would be announced if there was to be a raid that night. Soon, the ground crew were busy checking each aircraft's radar, guns, engines, etc and filling the wing tanks with over 2,000 gallons of fuel. Armourers would load the guns with ammunition and bring up and mount a mix of high-explosive and incendiary bombs in the bomb bays for that night's target. (The bombs were stored in a remote part of the airfield for safety, behind blast walls. They would be fused for the target and towed on long low trolleys, by tractor, to the aircraft dispersal points.) Although the target was not disclosed at this stage, because of the strict security rules, ground crews would have a good idea from the amount of fuel loaded and the type of bombload, of where the target was to be.

About the same time as the ground crew were engaged in these activities, aircrew would be briefed by their respective leaders. There would be a leader for each discipline, e.g. pilots, navigators, bomb aimers etc. The navigators would be some of the busiest; the navigation leader would issue them with flight plans and meteorological information. They would be the first to know the target and would then plot the route on their chart and smaller topographical maps highlighting towns, lakes and rivers near to their track. Initial courses and airspeeds would be calculated from the wind velocities supplied (these would be modified as more information was gained from Gee and H2S during the flight). It was essential that navigators kept to their prescribed altitudes, tracks and timetable, to maintain the concentration of the bomber stream and in order to keep to their time slot over the target, which was no more than three minutes long.

The aircrew would then go to the mess, have their operational meal of eggs and bacon (civilians were lucky to get one egg a month!), and fill their Thermos flasks with coffee. They would draw their flying rations of chocolate and orange juice to sustain them during the long night, and would also have available caffeine tablets to keep them alert.

The squadron briefing would then follow, when all the aircrew due to be on operational duty that night (about 150 personnel) were assembled in front of a large wall map of Europe, showing the route and the target. If it was to be the 'Big City' (Berlin) a gasp would go round the hut, as it was considered to be the most dangerous target of them all. The briefing was carried out by the squadron commander, the intelligence officer, the meteorology officer and any other specialist whose views were pertinent to that night's raid. The briefing would cover overall details of the operation such as:

1. The size of the bombing force and the objective of any diversionary raids taking place.
2. The weather expected en route and when returning to base; the forecast wind changes; the extent of cloud en route and over the target, and icing risks at various altitudes.
3. How the Pathfinders would be marking the route and target.
4. The danger spots for flak and night fighters.

Finally, all personnel, especially navigators, were asked to synchronise their watches (to the second) to GMT.

After this, the aircrew drew their parachutes and 'Mae Wests', left any personal items in a bag to be picked up if and when they returned, and departed by truck to their dispersal points around the airfield. At the dispersal point they had time to smoke a cigarette outside the aircraft (not frowned upon in those days), and then to check their equipment thoroughly before they took off. The air gunners checked their guns over the North Sea.

At times, crews would get to this point of preparation and have to wait for the clearance of fog. The 'met' officer would have guaranteed that it would clear, but sometimes it did not, and the operation would then have to be abandoned.

At last, it was time to take off and crews were directed by the airfield controller to the runway, where many of the ground crew would wave them off into the gathering darkness. Then commenced the long ordeal (five to eight hours) of freezing cold, and the heavy vibration and incessant roar of four Rolls-Royce Merlin engines, in an unpressurised aircraft, until they returned (with luck, unscathed) in the early hours of the following morning. On their return, crews went to the debriefing hut, where they were given hot coffee and a tot of rum dispensed by the padre. This was followed by a debriefing by an intelligence officer, who took notes about the bombing run and any details of flak and night fighters that aircrews had encountered during the night. After an egg and bacon breakfast, they trekked back to their respective Nissen huts, crawled into bed, and attempted to get some sleep, if that was at all possible, and await the next call.

After ten days of cross-country flights at Pocklington as Squadron Leader Harvey's crew, and after practising with Gee and H2S equipment, we were considered ready for our first operation. This was a mine-laying trip (described as 'gardening and planting vegetables') to the coastal waters on the east side of Denmark. Mine-laying was regarded as a reasonably safe and easy task and was therefore considered suitable for a crew's first mission. However, this turned out not to be so in our case!

On 2 October 1943 we took off, carrying in the bomb bay two mines and their parachutes. Some 117 aircraft took part, mining various places from Lorient to Heligoland. We climbed on track across the North Sea to a height of 10,000 feet. About halfway across the North Sea, S/L Harvey asked Laurie to take over the controls while he visited the toilet at the rear of the aircraft. Laurie, as bomb aimer, would have had some training to assist the pilot on take-off, but not in flying the plane. In fact, Laurie had never sat in the pilot's seat of a Halifax before.

In the event, Laurie was asked to fly the plane on his first operation and, even worse, as we approached the enemy coast – S/L Harvey really must have had an urgent call of nature! If the rest of us had really grasped the magnitude of what Laurie had been asked to do, then I think we would all have needed to 'go', as well. Luckily for everyone, S/L Harvey was back in his place before we crossed the Danish coast.

However, on passing over the coast there was a loud bang, which lifted the aircraft up alarmingly, although soon afterwards the plane restored itself to level flight. At this point, both the 'Gee' and 'H2S' navigation systems went out of action, but we continued across Denmark to our dropping zone, described as the 'Samso Belt', which we identified visually through broken cloud.

The bomb doors were opened, and we made our dropping run at 8,000 feet. We then attempted to release the mines, but they would not drop. Several attempts were made to liberate them manually, but without success. S/L Harvey then decided to return to base with the mines on board and tried to close the bomb doors; these would not shut. It was now evident that the hydraulic system had been damaged, as well as the radar equipment, probably caused by a flak ship as we crossed the Danish coast earlier.

We reduced our height to 2,000 feet to get under the cloud base and experienced some nasty electric storms across the North Sea. This was necessary, though, as, without the technical navigational aids, I had to pick out landfall as soon as possible, having only 'dead reckoning' as a means of navigation.

As we did not need oxygen at this height, I decided at this point to visit the Elsan toilet at the rear of the aircraft. Taking a torch, I groped my way to the back in the darkness. I was just stepping over the main spar, when by torchlight I noticed a gaping hole beneath me; had I completed the step I would have fallen 2,000 feet into the North Sea without a parachute – I relieved myself through the hole! I returned to the nose section immediately to confirm to S/L Harvey that there was no doubt that we had been hit by flak. I then had a drink of coffee from my Thermos flask to restore my shattered nerves.

It was now obvious that the damage was more serious than we had first thought. Loss of hydraulic power meant that, not only were the bomb doors down, but when the flaps and wheels were lowered for landing, the bomb doors, flaps and wheels could not be raised again. If we were to overshoot the runway on landing, we would crash – with two mines still on board!

These thoughts kept us silent, with all eyes skinned for our landfall, Flamborough Head on the Yorkshire coast, and the sight of the flashing pundit that would indicate the close proximity of our airfield. Luckily, my dead reckoning navigation brought us back home on course, and we landed safely, otherwise these notes would not have been written! On landing, one of the mines fell out on to the runway. At our dispersal point the ground staff were amazed that, in such circumstances, we had survived as a crew without a scratch.

Both the mines, their release mechanism, the bomb doors and the fuselage had been damaged by shrapnel, and the parachutes badly torn. The hydraulics were severed, and the Gee and H2S were also damaged. Above the flak hole, we discovered that the fuselage was peppered with shrapnel holes, within inches of the mid-upper gunner's turret.

We were originally told that the aircraft would be written off, but I have learned since then that the aircraft was repaired. It carried out a number of missions, including to targets such as Kassel and Berlin, but, sadly, it was shot down by a night fighter off Denmark in April 1944, again on a mine-laying operation. All the crew died when the aircraft crashed into the sea. This same crew had saved their lives three months beforehand, coincidentally on the night we were shot down, having baled out of their Halifax, which was short of petrol. Such was the fragility of life in Bomber Command at that time.

Reading the squadron's Operations Record after the war, I found S/L Harvey's statement on our mine-laying mission to be totally inaccurate.

There was no mention of flak damage and having to bring the mines back, although the Pocklington Station Operations Record did report it accurately. I believe that S/L Harvey wanted to have a successful tour of operations on his record, and a possible DFC award later on!

Having had a near miss with shrapnel close to his turret, the mid-upper gunner decided to report sick before the next operation. In fact, he never flew again, and sadly he was labelled LMF (Lack of Moral Fibre), reduced from sergeant to AC2, and posted to Elvington (one of our affiliated airfields) for general duties. Such arbitrary action was taken by commanding officers as a deterrent to all aircrew to do as he had done.

At this time, losses in aircrew were extremely high, so much so that one crew hardly ever got to know another one, before one of the two crews went missing. A missing crew would first be noticed by other crews, when a number of beds became vacant in one's Nissen hut. Every operation to Germany, especially to places such as Berlin, was akin to 'going over the top' in the First World War. A succession of such stressful raids could bring on exhaustion and a fit of nerves to anyone, however strong in body and mind. The threat of being branded LMF was made to avoid the eventuality where aircrew would refuse to fly. In point of fact only about 0.4% of all aircrew in Bomber Command were branded as LMF during the entire war. Nevertheless, some who had lived through as many as twenty operations before they ceased flying, were cashiered or demoted with ignominy. This was a huge injustice, especially when one considers that there were many civilians of military age, in reserved occupations, who would never be exposed to such risks. In addition, a large proportion of servicemen in all the armed services would never have to face such an exceptionally high risk of death on every operational mission. Bomber Command was unique.

As the mine-laying mission was my first operation, and because of the experiences I had had on that flight, the squadron navigation officer decided to check through my log and chart. He found both completely accurate and commended me on the results, which he knew were made under testing conditions. Later he informed me that he was recommending me for a commission. Actually, this was long overdue and should have been made at the time I qualified as a navigator in Canada, when I had failed to 'make the grade' by a few marks.

Chapter 3

Further Ops

Our next operation was on 4 October 1943, to Frankfurt. This was not a success as, firstly S/L Harvey had decided to weave all the way to Germany (not normally done unless there is some predicted flak, or there are night fighters about).It certainly made the navigator's job more difficult! Secondly, without explanation, the pilot turned back to base, dropping our bombs into the North Sea on the way home. We had flown five hours out of about seven to complete the bombing operation, and had been less than 100 miles from the target when we turned back.

S/L Harvey reported in the squadron Operations Record: 'Overload petrol pump U/S. Returned early.' I had a feeling that S/L Harvey wasn't very happy about flying that night, after our mine-laying experiences just two days beforehand. However, it was frustrating for us, having got so near the target, as this raid turned out to be the first serious blow to Frankfurt so far in the war. Later, the flight engineer went sick and as far as I can recall he did not fly again.

Our third operation was on 8 October 1943, this time to Hanover, when 504 aircraft took part. This mission proceeded without mishap. We had no trouble en route, it was clear over the target, we bombed on the red target indicators (the Pathfinder markers) from 17,200 feet, and fires were seen to start at the target point. This raid was reported as the most successful attack on Hanover of the war. We began to think that we would at last be successful as a crew, but this proved not to be so.

Apart from a cross-country flight and an air test, we did not fly on any more operations in October. In fact, we did not fly any more missions again with S/L Harvey, although officially he remained the 'A' Flight commander until the end of November 1943.

Shortly after our third operation, I was interviewed by Air Commodore 'Gus' Walker for my commission. During that meeting he informed me that S/L Harvey was being withdrawn from operational flying, indicating that he had had enough. This did not really surprise me, especially as Bomber Command had now entered a phase when life was becoming very fragile indeed. What did amaze me, however, was to learn, much later, that at the end of November 1943, when he relinquished command of 'A' Flight, S/L Harvey was recommended for a DFC. The award was described as 'long overdue' for his tours in the Middle East in 1941 and his operations over Germany. The latter included one in June 1942, and two with us in October 1943, which included the 'returned early' operation. He was awarded the DFC on 28 December 1943.

Now we were a headless crew all over again, awaiting the posting of another pilot. In the meantime, we were destined to fly as spares, replacing crew members in other crews who were sick or otherwise unable to fly. This was a very demoralising position to be in. As a regular crew, you developed a team spirit and trust in each other. Your lives were in each other's hands. Although this was also true when flying in a crew as a 'spare', you were just a floating part. You usually had little or no faith in the crew you were joining for that night and, for that matter, neither were they likely to have any faith in you. The lack of trust in this situation was bad for the morale of the whole crew.

On one occasion I complained to the acting 'A' Flight commander about flying as a spare. His reply was: 'You will probably carry on like it, until one day you just don't come back.' Later, I checked up on the progress of his career and found that he survived his first tour and got a DFC at the end of May 1944. I have often wondered whether or not he survived the rest of the war.

Laurie Underwood (bomb aimer), John Bushell (rear gunner) and I (navigator) then flew as spares for the next five or so operations, which was one of the most unnerving periods I can remember. Our wireless operator seemed to have disappeared, so we were now down to three of our original crew.

More than a month had elapsed since I had flown on the Hanover operation, before my next mission on 11 November 1943. This was a mine-laying operation off the Frisian Islands (near the Dutch coast). I flew with F/O Eddy, and forty-five aircraft took part on the 'op'. We dropped our mines from 6,000 feet and we lost one aircraft from our squadron, shot down by a flak ship. The aircraft ditched in the North Sea, with all the crew missing, presumed killed. This was the same aircraft in which I had flown with S/L Harvey when we went to Frankfurt and returned early on 4 October 1943.

My fifth operation was on 18 November , to Mannheim/Ludwigshafen, flying as a spare with P/O Jackson, an Australian pilot. Some 395 aircraft took part. It was a raid to divert German night fighters away from the main force of bombers, who were striking Berlin. We attacked from 17,000 feet on the green target indicators – the bombing was well concentrated. The diversion was successful in that the main force only suffered 2% losses, whereas our losses were high, at 5.8%. However, 102 Squadron did not lose any aircraft that night.

I flew again as spare with F/O Jackson on 22 November to the 'Big City' – Berlin – the most heavily defended city in Germany; 764 aircraft took part, dropping 2,501 tons of incendiaries and high explosives in about twenty minutes. This was the second of sixteen raids to be described as the Battle of Berlin. For all raids, the target was the centre of Berlin (Hitler's Chancery), and for each raid the city was approached from a different point of the compass. Unless Pathfinders directed us to do otherwise, bombing on each raid would 'creep back' like a wedge from the target point; thus the whole city would be covered by bombing over the period of the sixteen raids.

This night, our bombing run was from the west, and we bombed at 18,000 feet on the centre of the flares (checked by H2S). The glow from the fires were seen through 9/10ths cloud cover. This raid was the third heaviest of the war on Berlin and it was also the most successful. Much damage was done to industrial areas and munitions factories, to the Ministry of Weapons and Munitions and to many political and administrative buildings. The Kaiser Wilhelm Memorial Church was also badly damaged. (After the war, it was partly restored and partly rebuilt, and became a Berlin tourist attraction. It can be compared with Coventry Cathedral, which, back in 1940, had been gutted by the Luftwaffe, when they devastated the city. Following the hostilities, a new cathedral was built alongside the ruins of the old, just as was the case in Berlin, to serve as a permanent reminder of the horror of total war).

After the raid on 22 November, the equivalent of nearly three German Army divisions were drafted in to tackle the fires and clear the damage, which extended from the centre to the western limits of the city. Luckily we had experienced no night-fighter attacks or flak damage on this raid, but we narrowly missed having an accident on our return to Pocklington. While we were still on the outer circuit waiting to land, another Halifax from our squadron, flying on the same outer circuit as ourselves, had collided head-on with a Halifax from 77 Squadron. It had been returning to our affiliated airfield at Full Sutton, and was also on its outer circuit preparing to land. The two outer circuits unfortunately overlapped, and as a result of the mid-air collision, both crews were killed outright – we had missed the same fate by a small margin. John Bushell (the rear gunner in our crew, who was also now flying as a spare) had the unenviable task of representing 102 Squadron at the funeral of one of those who was killed.

I continued my time as spare, flying with F/O Jackson. His navigator must have had a long time off for sickness, or for some other reason, and was not flying. On our next raid, on 25 November 1943, our target was Frankfurt, and only 262 aircraft took part. The flight was uneventful, although the gunners had heated discussions about seeing night fighters, until F/O Jackson, in his casual Australian voice, settled the argument by saying: 'If they've only got two engines, shoot the bastards down!' We bombed on the red target indicators from 17,500 feet. Some fires were seen, but it was cloudy over the target and the bombing appeared to be scattered. Despite the small force of aircraft out on that mission, 102 Squadron managed to lose two aircraft over Germany, keeping up its record of high losses.

We had hardly got to bed after the debriefing from the Frankfurt raid in the early hours of 26 November, when the tannoys blared out for all aircrew to report to their sections to be briefed for another raid that night. We were supplied with caffeine tablets and given 'pink gins' to drink, in the hope that it would keep us 'on our toes' that night. I flew again with F/O Jackson in a small force of 178 aircraft to Stuttgart. This was a diversionary raid to draw off German night fighters from the main force of bombers, whose target was, yet again, Berlin. We bombed on the red target indicators from 17,500 feet. Large fires were seen and bombing was scattered but, as planned, a part of the German night-fighter force was successfully drawn off from the main bomber force. We lost one aircraft, which crashed near Pocklington, and one that came back badly damaged by a night fighter, and whose rear gunner was killed.

On our return we were diverted to Hartford Bridge airfield in the south, so that the main force of Lancasters could use 4 Group airfields, as some of their airfields were fog bound. They were also short of petrol after an exceptionally long flight. Nevertheless, fourteen Lancasters crashed in England that night. We returned to Pocklington after a weekend in Hartford Bridge, on three engines after one engine failed on take-off.

This was my last flight with F/O Jackson, who was awarded the DFM. He finished his tour and was given the DFC in June 1944 – perhaps I should have stayed with him rather than return to my original crew!

Before Laurie Underwood, John Bushell and I came together again as a crew, I had just one other experience when I was due to fly as a spare. Fortunately the pilot, prior to take-off, taxied off the concrete dispersal point into the mud of the outfield and the flight had to be abandoned. Just as well, as I had had premonitions about flying that night with that particular crew.

The month of December 1943 proved to be one of non-activity, because at first there was a full moon, and then the weather was poor. I was also waiting for a week's leave to get my officer's uniform (my promotion, although it had been approved, had not yet been promulgated) and we were awaiting the names of those who were to complete our crew. Eventually, we learned who they were:

Pilot	F/O G.A. Griffiths, DFM: 'Griff'	(On his second tour)
Second dickey pilot	Sgt. K.F. Stanbridge	(Observational flight, to gain experience)

Flight engineer	Sgt J. Bremner	(Had done previous ops)
Wireless operator	F/S E.A. Church	(Had done previous ops)
Mid-upper gunner	F/S C.G. Dupueis (French Canadian)	(Had done previous ops – spare crew)

It seemed beyond belief that our new flight commander did not authorise any cross-country 'runs' for us to gain crew experience, or to practise H2S, bombing and gunnery procedures, before we flew on operations together. However, it was not to be, and on 29 December we were scheduled on a main force operation to Berlin.

This was the eighth raid on Berlin and the fifth heaviest – 712 aircraft took part, and 2,314 tons of incendiaries and high explosives were dropped in twenty minutes. It was an uneventful flight. I remember clearly seeing the outline of the Zuider Zee on the radar screen (H2S was always at its best on coastal outlines) as we flew over northern Holland. Bad weather restricted the German night fighters to sixty-six, but these were the more experienced crews with air interception and H2S homing radar and upward-firing cannon. Fortunately, due to two spoof raids by RAF Mosquitoes, the night fighters reached Berlin too late to be effective.

We flew into Berlin from the south-east and dropped our bombs from 17,500 feet on the target indicators, but no results were seen, owing to 10/10ths cloud cover. Aircraft losses that night were down to 2.8%, but 102 Squadron yet again managed to beat the average, with two aircraft missing. In one of these aircraft, Harold Paar, a Chigwell neighbour of mine, was shot down on his first operation. He later became a POW in the same camp as me – Stalag IVB – and in the same hut. (I discovered that he was a neighbour of mine, when my son met Harold's son in the same grammar school class, some twenty years later!)

Chapter 4

Into the Dark

January 1944 began as another month of inactivity, again as a result of bad weather, and a full moon, the combination of which led to a reluctance to send Halifax IIs out to Berlin, because of their increasing vulnerability. However, another maximum effort to attack Berlin was required, so our second operation, as full crew again, was scheduled for Berlin on 20 January 1944. As well as our 'normal' crew of seven, a second pilot, Sgt K.F. Stanbridge (flying as a second dickey pilot for operational experience), was again included, making us up to a crew of eight.

For this operation I was responsible as one of four navigators operating H2S equipment in 4 Group. No. 4 Group comprised 15 squadrons totalling 250–300 aircraft. My duty was to radio at intervals my calculated wind velocities back to 4 Group. These wind velocities from the four navigators were to be averaged and rebroadcast to the whole of 4 Group for their use in maintaining concentration in the bomber stream. In addition, I was to do my own blind bombing that night (not bombing on Pathfinder markers), using H2S to identify the homing point for a timed run into Berlin.

This bombing raid on 20 January was to be the ninth raid and the fourth heaviest on Berlin; 769 aircraft took part and 2,400 tons of incendiary and high-explosive bombs were dropped in twenty minutes. The raid was considered to have been successful, although less concentrated than planned. Due to bad weather again over Germany, the German night fighters were limited to ninety-eight experienced crews equipped with 'Schräge Musik' – upward-firing cannon – radar interception and H2S homing devices. The night fighters (all twin-engined) were also operating a new procedure called 'tame boar', where they were directed by ground control into the bomber stream at intervals and over the target. From this point, they could fly freelance and use their own equipment to seek out bombers, fly beneath them out of sight of the bombers' gunners, and fire cannon shells into their petrol-laden wings. Additionally, on this night, thin cloud covering Berlin, with tops at about 12,000 feet, was illuminated from below by many searchlights, allowing the night fighters flying above the bomber stream to locate them, silhouetted against this bright backcloth. Thus, despite the limitations of night fighters, it was a highly successful night for them, as they claimed thirty-three victories (nine of them over Berlin) out of the thirty-five bombers lost that night.

We took off at 1630 hours GMT on 20 January in a Halifax nicknamed 'Old Flo' by the ground crew, and were soon flying above 10/10ths cloud. Using Gee radar initially, and then H2S to 'map read', we flew uninterrupted over a northerly route into Germany, turning south-east about 60 miles from Berlin. Berlin is a large city and there were too many stray reflections on the H2S screen to be able to identify the target position. I was instructed personally at the navigators' briefing in Pocklington to identify a turning point, by taking a precise bearing and distance on my H2S screen, of a small town about 10 miles north of Berlin. This was the commencement of a timed bombing run to the target – Hitler's Chancery. We flew in straight and level at 18,000 feet, maintaining a pre-calculated track and groundspeed, and at the time set by stop watch we dropped our bombs, at 2000 hours GMT.

This bombing procedure made us a sitting target for the night-fighter expertise available that night, for we had hardly closed our bomb doors when we were hit by one of these aircraft. He had trailed behind and below our Halifax, waiting for our bombs to be released, then fired cannon shells upwards into our starboard wing. With more than 1,000 gallons of petrol still aboard, it was only seconds before the whole wing was aflame.

I hear 'Griff', our pilot, cry out: 'Graviners, engineer!' (The graviners were switches to activate the engine fire extinguishers.) This was to no avail, and the blaze was so fierce that 'Griff' realised that the aircraft was stricken, and immediately called out: 'Parachute, parachute, bale out!'

I was already wearing my parachute, and also had my seat and my navigator's table folded back clear of the escape hatch (a discipline I always observed when over a target, when we were at our most vulnerable). I lifted the escape-hatch door and dropped it diagonally through the hatch itself, but it caught the slipstream and jammed half in and half out of the aircraft. With my efforts, combined with those of the wireless operator, Eric Church, and Laurie Underwood, the bomb aimer, we managed to kick the errant door clear. I sat on the edge of the escape hatch and dropped through immediately, followed closely by Laurie. It was truly a leap of faith – a leap into the dark, with fingers and toes crossed, as we had no idea what would happen next. The wireless operator had no time to follow us, and perished with the plane. I believe that, after Laurie dropped out, the blazing aircraft went out of control and into a spiral dive.

After baling out at 17,000 feet, I spun over a few times, and then pulled the ripcord. The canopy opened and my harness tightened with a jerk around my crotch, which brought me to my senses in double quick time! Below me and to my left, I could see another parachute; it might have been Laurie's but I couldn't be sure. We didn't meet again until his wedding after the war.

Meanwhile, I was over a layer of light cloud, and was aware of the glow of fires beneath it. Coming up were plenty of heavy flak and tracer shells, hose-piping around the sky – I prayed they wouldn't come too near!

I floated earthwards for ten to fifteen minutes; somehow I didn't feel too cold, although it would have been about minus 34° Celsius when I jumped out. With a 60-mph northerly wind prevailing, I soon drifted away from being near to the centre of the city. The deafening noise from the aircraft's engines, present during the flight, had gone, and now the sound of bursting flak had died away too. Instead there was an uncanny silence, and the blackness of the night, as I descended through the cloud that covered the area. Nearing the ground, I thought I was going to land in marshes, and my hand was on the lever to inflate my 'Mae West' life jacket, but it turned out to be the tops of the trees in a small wood in a southern suburb of Berlin. I crashed through these, falling the last 15 feet, and finished up with only a grazed face and a sprained ankle. It was remarkable that this was the only injury I sustained throughout this ordeal.

In fewer than twenty minutes, my life had gone through a dramatic change. I had survived death by a hair's breadth. I was elated at being alive, but what of my crew – were they alive or dead? What traumas would my family suffer when they were informed by telegram that I was missing, at sometime tomorrow morning? A few hours beforehand I had been eating my eggs and bacon (only available before operational flights) in the mess at Pocklington with my aircrew colleagues around me; the friendly town of York was only 12 miles away, and home leave to get my officer's kit was imminent.

I was now in hostile Germany, probably in the south-eastern suburbs of Berlin. What would happen if I were caught by civilians, having just bombed their city? There was nobody here who would care whether I lived or died. Germany was now in the depths of winter. I was in enemy territory, 600 miles from home, with only some French francs, a hand-kerchief with a map of France printed on it, and a magnetic trouser button with a white spot on it, which, when cut off my flies and balanced on a pencil point, would point north! Oh, and a tin of Horlick's tablets. I had only these to sustain me, while I evaded capture and made my way back to England. Added to this, I was a still in my flight sergeant's uniform (although I had been commissioned on 1 December 1943), and I was five days away from my twenty-first birthday.

About eight hours later, having disturbed a dog while trying to hide in a barn, I was captured by the civilian police. The story from this point onwards until the end of the war is told in the following pages.

But what of my crew members? Laurie had 'blacked out', I believe, during part of his parachute drop, but landed uninjured, and was captured by the military early the next day. Out of our crew of eight, only four came through the ordeal. The other two survivors, 'Griff', the pilot, and John Bushell, the rear gunner, had had the most remarkable of escapes from death!

After Laurie and I baled out, and the aircraft had gone into a spiral dive, 'Griff' was thrown forward towards the controls. He was held in his seat by the 'G' force of the spiral dive. He saw the altimeter unwind past 7,000 feet, and wondered when his end would come, before losing consciousness. I believe that the petrol tanks of the blazing aircraft exploded, and 'Griff' was blown out, regaining consciousness just in time to pull his ripcord, a few hundred feet from the ground. His parachute was still on the swing when he thumped down among debris from the aircraft on waste ground in Berlin. He was uninjured, but in shock. He wrapped himself up in his parachute and went to sleep under a bush nearby, where he was discovered the next morning by a party of civilians, led by a soldier.

John was thrown over his guns when the aircraft went into the spiral dive, and he also lost consciousness. He 'came to' in the air, in similar circumstances to 'Griff', and opened his parachute near the ground, but he landed close to a searchlight battery and was captured immediately. John had a bad cut over his right eye and a bruised face, but was otherwise all right.

Strangely enough, the four crew who were killed were those who were fairly new to us. The wireless operator and co-pilot were eventually buried in the British War Cemetery in Berlin. When he had been captured, 'Griff', our pilot, was asked by the German military: 'Tell us the name of your wireless operator, so that we can bury him with a name.' The flight engineer and the mid-upper gunner were neither found nor identified, and, having no known graves, were remembered only on the War Memorial at Runnymede.

It was very sad that the mid-upper gunner, F/S C.G. Dupueis, had avoided an assignment to Berlin on his thirteenth operation by flying on a comparatively 'safe' mission instead, only to be killed on this raid to Berlin, his fourteenth operation. The lucky rabbit's foot that he always carried with him did not help him on this occasion. I also regret that I had said to the wireless operator, F/S E.A. Church, before this op, that he shouldn't take milk from the sergeant's mess for his own use. I had not known then that he had taken it for his young wife, who was living near Pocklington, and who was expecting a baby. (I was destined to meet that 'baby' later on, in 2008 – see Chapter 16).

After the war, we survivors came to realise that 20 January 1944 was a night to remember, having been recorded by both sides as one of unprecedented activity. Some fifty years later we learned, through a German archivist, that we had been shot down by an ace night-fighter pilot, Hauptmann L. Fellerer, in a twin-engined Messerschmitt Bf110

G4 night fighter. He had forty-one victories to his credit, had been awarded the Knight's Cross, and had shot down five aircraft, including ours, on that night. He became Gruppen Kommandor of the Night Fighter Group 11/NJG5 at Parchim near Berlin. Following the hostilities, he became a high-ranking officer in the Austrian Air Force, but was killed in a Cessna flying accident in July 1968.

The German archivist had also provided a map of Berlin, showing approximately where our aircraft had crashed, which was about 7 miles south-east of Hitler's Chancery, at Oberspree. This confirms that we were on target that night, as the crash point was on our track, less than two minutes' flying distance from the time we had released our bombs.

The date of 20 January 1944 was a significant one for 102 Squadron, as the extract from the squadron's Operations Record summary shows (microfilm held at the Public Records Office, Kew):

Weather foggy clearing later, Vis: mod to good. Wind s'ly 20–25 mph.

16 Aircraft detailed to attack Berlin on what proved to be probably the most disastrous operation embarked upon by the Squadron, which suffered the loss of 5 crews missing (F/O Griffiths DFM, PO Dean, F/S Render, W/O Wilding, & F/S Compton). Moreover, two aircraft were lost in this country, F/O Hall (short of petrol, had to abandon his aircraft near Driffield, the whole crew baling out successfully). F/S Proctor crash landed near Norwich, the Airbomber F/O Turnbull unfortunately dying from his injuries. The rest of the crew suffered minor injuries as a result. Thus no fewer than 7 of the 16 aircraft which took off were lost, including 5 crews – fortunately, an exceptional night of misfortune and unlikely to be repeated. There was also one early return; F/O W.B. Dean, or 'W'.

So that was the end of our time in Bomber Command. After re-forming as a full crew again following our time as spares, we had accomplished only two more operations, making, for me, only ten operations in all:

1.   2 October 1943:   Mine-laying (Denmark)

2. 4 October 1943:   Frankfurt
3. 8 October 1943:   Hanover
4. 11 November 1943:   Mine-laying (Frisian Islands)
5. 18 November 1943:   Ludwigshaven
6. 22 November 1943:   Berlin
7. 25 November 1943:   Frankfurt
8. 26 November 1943:   Stuttgart
9. 29 December 1943:   Berlin
10. 20 January 1944:   Berlin

Nevertheless, we will go down in the annals of 102 Squadron as having been shot down on the night when the squadron suffered the loss of seven out of 16 operational aircraft, or 44% of the planes that flew that night, which was a loss greater than in any other operation in the squadron's history in both world wars.

No. 102 Squadron was not a lucky squadron: after the disastrous night of 20 January 1944, another four aircraft were lost on the following night's raid to Magdeburg. Shortly after this, as the losses continued, the squadron was stood down from operations over Germany. Subsequently, the Halifax Mark IIs were withdrawn, to be replaced by the Halifax IIIs, which were equal to the Lancasters of that time in their operational efficiency.

Unfortunately for our crew, the new aircraft arrived too late, otherwise we might have had a better chance of survival, and we would have been able to complete at least one tour – thirty operations –and perhaps we would even have been able to avoid ending up in captivity for the rest of the war.

In the Second World War, 102 Squadron suffered the highest losses in 4 Group Bomber Command (fifteen squadrons), and the third highest losses in the whole of Bomber Command (ninety-three squadrons).

Part Two
Captivity

Reg Wilson. POW official ID
photograph. Late January 1944.

Chapter 5

My Capture

Parachuting from 17,000 feet in a strong north-westerly wind meant that it was about seventeen minutes before I landed, luckily well away from the bombed area of Berlin, in a quiet leafy place. I had descended through cloud, and crashed through trees in a small wood in a suburb to the south of Berlin. I was amazed to find that I had sustained no injuries, apart from a grazed face and a sprained ankle. I released my parachute and removed my Mae-West life jacket. These I hid from sight as best I could, and made my way to the edge of the wood.

I was now on the edge of a tree-lined street of suburban houses, and I could hear the voices of two or three people as they walked along the street. Somehow, I did not feel scared, but nevertheless I dodged behind trees as they passed by. I think that the enormity of the occasion, and the fact that I had survived almost without a scratch, had filled me with some kind of elation at that time (although I had no idea whether any of the rest of the crew were alive or dead).

I proceeded furtively along the street, and then quite suddenly I felt an urgent call of nature, and I had to find a spot where I could immediately relieve myself. This was in somebody's front garden. I have often wondered since, what would have happened if I had been discovered in this position by a local resident, especially as I had just bombed their city.

The street led out into a country road, with houses scattered along it, and I decided that this was the best route to follow, as I might find a farm building where I could hide for the time being. It was now night-time, in January, and although cold, it was dry, and I did not feel too much discomfort, apart from my sprained ankle.

I walked on through the night. As soon it would be getting light, I needed to 'hole up' somewhere. I turned off the road towards a barn and unfortunately disturbed a dog, which started to bark. Almost from nowhere, an old man appeared. Apparently, he was 'knocking up' his workers. Farm workers started early in Germany, as they did everywhere else. He saw me, and he said 'kaputt', and I nodded. I could have knocked him down, but I decided that discretion was the better part of valour. As I was near the Berlin suburbs in Germany, and not in Holland or in France, where some help from the local population might be possible, any resistance here (so far east, and in enemy territory) could end in disaster for me.

The old man telephoned from the farm, and shortly afterwards two policemen appeared, one brandishing a revolver and a pair of handcuffs. The latter indicated to me that if I walked with them they would not handcuff me, but if I started to run away, they would shoot me. As by now my sprained ankle was causing me trouble, I hobbled alongside them back to one of their houses, where I was exhibited to the policeman's wife before I was taken to the police station.

At the police station I was searched, and all my (few) possessions – my wallet, cigarette case, navigation watch, escape gear, French francs, a map of Europe on a handkerchief, and a tin of Horlicks tablets – were taken from me. They did not discover my special metal trouser button, which pointed north when balanced on a pencil point, and was sewn to my flies!

They opened my wallet, which contained only photos, and asked me quite courteously, by means of the odd word or gesture, whether I was married. They were quite impressed at the quality of my uniform, which happened to be almost new. They also asked me whether I was a 'Jude' (Jew). I often wondered what they would have done if I had said 'Yes'. After that, I was put in a cell in a yard at the rear of the station.

My stay at the police station was not uneventful. Firstly, through the high cell window grille, a French foreign worker said that 'Sept cama-rades sont morts.' As I still had no idea what had happened to my other seven crew members, this news was not helpful to my morale. Then, an attractive German girl in high leather boots was brought to the cell door and talked to me in English. I do not recall whether she was practising her English or trying her hand at interrogation, but she did restore my morale! She was followed by a police officer, who appeared with my cigarette case and offered me one of my own cigarettes. I indicated that he should also take one. As these cigarettes were State Express 555 (a superior brand), it was a cordial meeting. He took me out of the cell, and we walked beyond the yard to a small field, where he showed me several rows of incendiary bombs laid out, all marked with ICI lot numbers – obviously from some stricken bomber.

Sometime later, a sandwich was brought to me, wrapped in newspaper. This newspaper showed a large photograph of an American airman who had been shot down. The words 'Murder Incorporated' were painted on the back of his leather flying jacket. These words were used by the Italian Mafia in New York: the killer squads in the 1920s. The German press had lost no time in making use of this photograph, together with the headline 'Terrorflieger'. I wondered at the time whether or not the use of the newspaper 'wrapper' for my sandwich was accidental or deliberate. If it was deliberate, I was being labelled as being no better than the American, although the police otherwise behaved quite correctly towards me during my short sojourn at the police station.

It was late afternoon when I was moved from the police station, in an old Ford motorcar, which belched smoke all the way to a Luftwaffe airfield to the north-east of Berlin. As we approached the airfield, the police driver stopped to ask directions from two immaculately dressed Luftwaffe officers. One of them peered into the car and, looking at me, said, in perfect English, 'Last night?' I nodded and he said, 'We are night fighters', with a grin of satisfaction all over his face. In a few minutes we had arrived at the guard house of Werneuchen, a night-fighter station, one of several defending the city of Berlin.

I was soon locked in a guardhouse cell, awaiting the next event. Not long afterwards, I was taken to the officers' mess, and was paraded like a trophy in front of the commanding officer and company. The commanding officer indicated to me not to look so glum. I suppose he was thinking that, for me, the war was over, and I should be relieved that I was alright. I was returned to the cell, and the guardhouse sergeant came in and talked to me in broken English for some time. He had been a bomber pilot and had attacked London some sixty times in the latter part of 1941. I told him that I had been living in that part of London, and that now we were quits.

I remember that evening well. They brought in a large dish of macaroni milk pudding, which seemed to me like a feast, as I had had nothing (other than the rye bread sandwich), since my egg and bacon meal before we took off on the Berlin mission.

The following morning a corporal came into the cell. He could speak good English. He said that he was in the guardhouse as punishment for some misdemeanour, but I think he was planted to engage me in conversation. He talked about the war. He had been in the siege of Leningrad, and described the hardship that everyone had experienced there. He said that the Russians were almost subhuman, and were eating rats. He also claimed that the Russian hordes would overrun Europe if they were not stopped by the Western nations. Apparently he had been educated in England, and indicated that his best friend was an Englishman. I do not remember being asked anything controversial or being subjected to anything that could be construed as interrogation.

Later that day I was moved from Werneuchen, with three other RAF aircrew who had also been shot down, one being a wireless operator from my own squadron. We were being transferred to a Luftwaffe station at Spandau West, which involved travelling with only one Luftwaffe guard (who was armed, thankfully) on an underground train through the heart of Berlin, which was crowded with civilians. It was quite a worrying experience (like travelling the whole length of the Central Line in London), wondering whether they would suddenly turn into a lynch mob and start attacking us. We were extremely relieved when we arrived at Spandau West without incident.

The next two nights were spent in a bunker, as the RAF was still active in the area of Berlin. Our number increased to sixteen, but there was still no sign of any of my crew. However, I met yet another chap from my squadron, who had been shot down over Magdeburg (just west of Berlin) the night after me, and who had trained with me as a navigator in Canada.

Although up until then I had been relishing the sheer joy of being alive, I now began to reflect on my position. Had all my crew been killed? Would my parents have been notified by now that I was missing? If so, there would be weeks of agony for them before they learned that I was alive and uninjured. This was a time when all of us could finally talk to each other, and we talked our heads off about our narrow escapes and our capture. One chap had five pieces of shrapnel removed from his back while we were there.

The food we received in the bunker was poor, and was indicative of the sort of rations that we could expect as POWs. The rye bread was almost inedible – I don't think I ever got used to it the whole time I was a prisoner. Several of the chaps were in need of a smoke and tried to puff on straw from the bedding, wrapped in a small piece of newspaper! They kept worrying the guards for a cigarette, until one of the guards gave them one of his. I learned later that this guard had lost both his parents in a bombing raid just a short time beforehand … and yet he was prepared to spare us a cigarette. They weren't all monsters.

After two days, we were taken in a Luftwaffe bus to a railway terminus in Berlin. Our journey took us through the Tiergarten district of West Berlin. This area was the largest park in Berlin and not industrialised at all, and as such did not appear to be damaged very much. (Perhaps because of this the guards thought it was a good route to take.) As we approached the city centre, the damage was more widespread, and the Bismarckstrasse had certainly taken a hammering. On arrival at the railway station, our rather large party of guards hustled us directly on to the train bound for Frankfurt am Main, for which we were very thankful, as a number of Berliners on the platform started shouting and gesticulating at us in a threatening manner. The train reached Frankfurt the following morning, and we were taken by tram to the town of Oberursel – to Dulag Luft, the Luftwaffe interrogation centre.

On arrival we were all searched again and put in separate cells, with just our clothes and no possessions. The cells were entirely plain and featureless, with just a bed – a straw-filled paillasse – a chair and a small table. There was also an electric wall heater – not for our benefit, but for our discomfort, as it turned out.

So here I was, in solitary confinement, more or less in a void after all that had happened to me since leaving England. There was nobody to talk to, nothing to write with, no noise, nothing to see, just my thoughts to review over and over again.

It was almost a pleasure when an apparent civilian came into the cell. Of course, it was the 'Red Cross representative' about whom we had all been warned by our squadron! He had come in with a bogus Red Cross form to get all my details, starting with my name, my next of kin, and my squadron details etc. I said that, under the Geneva Convention, I was only allowed to give my name, rank and number, and after some discussion he left, having offered me a cigarette, which I took. Shortly after that, the electric heater came on and the cell began to get very hot, so hot in fact that I was able to smoulder a piece of straw from the paillasse to an ember (by poking it into the heater element) but unfortunately not enough to light the cigarette I had been given. The overheating was another ploy to unsettle us, because one couldn't sleep or relax at all, and the temperature could reach 120°F or more. The next day, I was taken to an interrogator, who was very polite and civilised. He started to talk about the war and then produced a photograph of the H2S radar equipment I had used for navigation and blind-bombing runs. He asked what it was, and I said I did not know. He then tried another tack, saying that I could be a spy, and they needed evidence to prove that I wasn't. I was then taken back to the cell to endure another hot day and night. During this time, the only food we got each day was just watery soup, rye bread spread with 'marg' or some sort of jam, and a drink of acorn coffee.

The following day was my twenty-first birthday, and I was taken back to the interrogator. He started off again, trying to get me to prove my identity. I persisted in quoting my name, rank and number, and in the end he got bored and produced a dossier of my squadron (102 Squadron), saying that we were one of their best customers! I was amazed that he had details of my squadron, and I would have dearly liked to have asked him whether any of my crew were alive. It was not until after the war that I learned that Dulag Luft was able to identify squadrons by the number painted on the side of the aircraft. Obviously, they were able to match the crew survivors to the close proximity of the aircraft wreckage. The interrogator was also accurate about numbers of prisoners, as 102 Squadron was the second highest squadron in the whole of Bomber Command, in terms of the numbers of POWs taken in Germany. After this episode, my grilling was over, and I asked the interrogator whether I could have a shave, as it was my twenty-first birthday. He duly arranged this for me.

The following morning I was transferred to the Dulag transit camp at Frankfurt am Main, and my few possessions were returned to me – except for my photographs and my cigarettes, which had been 'lost', and my astro-navigation watch, which had been confiscated under 'war regulations'. But for the watch I got an official receipt, which I still have, although the watch was never returned to me.

My interrogation period was about average in length, but some prisoners were in solitary confinement for many days. I can only assume that much depended on the 'intake' of prisoners. In January 1944, the losses to Bomber Command (and presumably the American Air Force) were high, about 10%. Because of the increasing numbers of prisoners and the limited number of cells, it may not have been possible for Dulag Luft to arrange longer periods of solitary confinement at this time.

I was overjoyed to meet John Bushell (my rear gunner) in the party when we were transferred to the transit camp. John had a bad cut over his right eye, which luckily had healed up reasonably well. After we were hit, the plane had gone into a spiral dive, causing him to hit his head on his guns, so he was in a dazed state. The plane exploded near the ground, and John only survived because he was blown out and able to open his parachute in time. He landed on a searchlight battery and was taken into custody immediately. I think he was twenty-four hours ahead of me in arriving at Dulag Luft. He told me that he had met Laurie Underwood (my bomb aimer, who followed me out of the aircraft) at Spandau in West Berlin. Laurie was captured by the Wehrmacht while he was walking west-wards through the night, away from Berlin. We also learned later that George Griffiths (our pilot) was safe, but we had no knowledge of the fate of the four remaining members of our crew. Details of George's survival and the fate of the four missing crew members were not known to me until after the end of the war.

At the Dulag transit camp we experienced a substantial change, which was to become critically important in our daily lives, in the form of the fantastic support of the International Red Cross (IRC). Without this organisation many would have died, or at least would have suffered ill health for the rest of their lives. We were now prisoners of war, but we would not be officially registered until we were moved to the next camp (although we had been photographed already with our RAF service numbers).

The transit camp, although under the control of the Luftwaffe, was run internally by a small group of RAF officers and sergeants (all aircrew prisoners of war). There were about 200 prisoners and we stayed there for two days. During this time, we were given essential clothing like boots, overcoats, and, almost unbelievably, a fibre case containing many items like, socks, underclothes, a sewing kit, cigarettes, tobacco, a pipe, chewing gum, soap, a toothbrush, a razor and even pyjamas! On baling out, some had lost their flying boots and had damaged clothing. It was, of course, winter, and no one had any other kit. All the aforementioned items were supplied through the International Red Cross. (At this time in the war, the items we received were mainly from America.)

The camp was well stocked with Red Cross food parcels and, together with the basic German rations, the 'RAF Staff' members were able to produce impressive meals in the communal mess. They were almost sumptuous considering that we had hardly eaten for a week or more. At this point, we were also able to send a postcard to our next of kin, which hopefully would get home in a month or so. I wrote: 'My Dear Mum & Dad, I am now in Germany. You cannot write until I reach a POW camp. Please keep in touch with the Red Cross. I am unhurt and quite well. Please tell Pat I am safe. Meanwhile do not worry at all. All my love, Reg.'

On departure, we were each given an American Red Cross food parcel. In some ways it was sad to leave the transit camp after such a dramatic change in our fortunes. But the camp was within a mile of Frankfurt's main railway station, and I knew that the town was due for more bombing attacks soon. In fact, seven weeks later the camp suffered severe damage, with some casualties, and had to be moved out of Frankfurt.

A large party of us was assembled and moved to the railway sidings, where we were put into 'cattle trucks' (presumably old French Army trucks) marked '8 chevaux 40 hommes', although there were more than forty of us to each truck. We were now in the hands of the Wehrmacht, and not the Luftwaffe. These trucks, with a few bales of straw added, were to be our living quarters for the next three days. Our fortunes had come down with a bump!

John and I had met neither Laurie nor George in the transit camp, and I can only assume that they were ahead of us and were already on their way to Stalag Luft III. I might have been with them, had my commission come through on time. As it was, John and I were travelling together on our way to Stalag IVB, Mühlberg am Elbe, a town about 30 miles east of

Leipzig and about 65 miles south of Berlin.

The journey to Stalag IVB was a nightmare. Each truck had an armed guard, standing by a partly opened door (for ventilation), but there was barely room to squat on the floor of the truck, let alone space for sleeping. There was one bucket for urinating in, slopping about in the straw in the centre of the truck. Occasionally the train would stop and we were allowed out in a long line, to drop our trousers and defecate beside the rail track. Our only pleasure was to enjoy some of the contents of our first food parcel (that which didn't need a tin opener!), together with a meagre portion of German black bread.

We arrived at Neuburxdorf railway sidings near Mühlberg – although we could not see the town – and we were ushered out on to the road about a mile or so from Stalag IVB. The scene looked like Siberia. There had been a recent fall of snow, which had partially thawed, and there was slush everywhere. Before us was a flat, desolate plain and just a blur in the distance, which was our destination.

Chapter 6

Stalag IVB, Mühlberg am Elbe

The road took us through the wide open space of fields to the east end of the prison camp, and we marched round it to the west gate. The camp was constructed at the end of 1939, and had then consisted mostly of tents, but these were eventually replaced with wooden barracks on either side of a main road, some being in separate compounds. Each area had a latrine to cope with forty prisoners at one 'sitting' – these were known as the forty-holers! There were various other buildings, including two cook-houses (for boiling mostly rotten potatoes and other root vegetables, and producing 'skilly' – watery soup – and acorn coffee). There were showers and delousing areas, and a hospital (of sorts). There were also several small compounds with solitary confinement cells to punish prisoners for breaking the rules, such as trying to escape. There were a number of water 'reservoirs', originally for supplying water for sewerage; this was planned but never completed. There was one particularly large one, with a windmill driving a water pump. These reservoirs were often referred to as the 'swimming pools', but were now stagnant and were presumably retained to be available in case of fire. Two compounds had space for sports activities and exercise (walking).

The camp was surrounded by a double barbed-wire fence with an inner trip wire. If you crossed this, you could be shot. There were six watchtowers, one at each corner, and one each in the centre of the two longer sides.

The camp initially housed French and Polish POWs, but by the end of 1944 it catered for the following nationalities: American (473), Belgian (66), British (7,578, including about 2,000 from the RAF), French (1,335), Italian (2,321), Dutch (1,269), Polish (2,455), Serbian (736), Slovakian

(652) and Russian (4,292) – totalling 21,177 prisoners in all.

Each wooden barracks was divided by a communal brick- and cement-built wash and boiler house. Each end catered for up to 250 prisoners, with only one inside night latrine. By 1944, as the war developed, due to the continual influx and transfer of prisoners, the barracks became dilapidated, cold and dismal, and massively overcrowded. The wooden exterior of the buildings – a dirty black/brown colour – were depressing to contemplate, especially in the snow, slush and mud of winter.

As we approached the west gate of the camp, we passed through the Wehrmacht administration and barracks block of our German guards. From here, we progressed on to a formidable wooden two-tower structure, with a bridge across the road and a sign bearing the inscription 'M STAMMLAGER IVB'. On' the bridge was a sentry box with a machine gun and a searchlight on top, and two patrolling guards. As we proceeded under the bridge, we knew that our lives were yet again going to change, and that entirely new experiences awaited us.

We moved into the showers and delousing block, where we were searched for the seventh time before we stripped off for a communal shower, while our clothing and possessions were passed through gas chambers (this was not lethal, I hasten to say). When our clothing was returned, it still smelt of gas, and I found that my flying boots (which were almost new) were missing. They had been 'appropriated' by the German or Russian helpers and I never saw them again. Instead I got a pair of ill-fitting clogs made of bits of leather upper, nailed to wooden soles. I had to clomp around in these for the next three months, in all the mud and slush, before I was finally given a pair of Army boots by the Red Cross.

After this experience, we moved to the 'hospital block', where we were literally stabbed with blunt needles by the French medical orderlies. These were our inoculation jabs against all the diseases that could result from the poor and insufficient food, the filthy conditions and the over-crowding which we would come to expect. The one disease the Germans were really afraid of was typhus as, the year before, an epidemic of typhus had wiped out many Russian prisoners, who were also working among civilians in the fields nearby. The Russians were considered dispensable, but the civilians were not.

We were registered as POWs on 1 February 1944, given a Stalag IVB number, and issued with our 'dog tags'. We also received two blankets apiece. Mine had obviously been used before, as they were very thin and had traces of having been soiled with excreta. Whether or not they had been laundered, I don't know, but they certainly had been through the gas chambers for delousing. Luckily, the one process that we were spared was having our heads shaved like convicts. We were the first 'intake' to escape this indignity – although, with shaved heads, we might have been in fashion, come another generation or so!

My first memory after registration was seeing the trail of British prisoners collecting their weekly Red Cross food parcels, although this was not always a full parcel and did not always arrive every week. We were quite lucky, as the camp, having had British prisoners since August 1943, was now benefiting from an established procedure under the Geneva Convention. The International Red Cross, operating from Switzerland, were the 'Protecting Power' (and so looked after the prisoners' welfare for Britain) and they dealt with the German Government, which was the 'Detaining Power'. British prisoners were represented by an elected 'Man of Confidence', who had contact with the German commandant about all matters arising day by day. Our 'Man of Confidence' was, in fact, a Canadian, whom we nicknamed 'Snowshoes'.

Compared with ourselves, the Russian prisoners were in a terrible state. Unlike us, they did not enjoy the protection of the Geneva Convention, and they had no Red Cross provision, and there was no repatriation of extremely sick or wounded soldiers. Those who were not sick or limbless had to work as slave labour (under Arbeitskommandos) in the fields and farms nearby. They were paid in 'Lagermarks' but these were relatively worthless. It was fortunate that they had the opportunity to 'trade' for bread etc with cigarettes obtained from POWs and, also, with the help of various 'rackets', were able to supplement their own meagre German rations. They were almost in rags, and the limbless and maimed were in a pitiful condition, reduced to begging and crawling in and out of incinerators for any scraps of food that might be remaining in tins. They were often in competition for these alongside stray dogs. The German guards gave the Russians no quarter and beat them at the slightest provocation. Of course, Germans who were taken prisoner on the Russian front were in the same position as the Russians, with no Geneva Convention to protect them.

Initially, we were housed with the British Army, who had originally been captured in North Africa before the Battle of El Alamein. They had been moved from Italian POW camps in July/August 1943 by the German Army, when the Italian front line in Italy was beginning to crumble. John Bushell and I were together, and we both appreciated the steadfastness of the British Army. They had been prisoners for a year or two already and were attuned to the lifestyle. They were resolute and disciplined, despite the fact that they had not been liberated in Italy, and had suffered poor treatment and lack of food under the Italians in their prison camps. As we had only left England eleven days beforehand, they wanted to know all the latest news from home.

Our first impression of the interior of the barracks was that they were abysmal. On the right-hand side were three tiers of rickety bunks in blocks of twelve, separated by a small corridor between each block. These continued up the right-hand side and some over to the left-hand side. In the centre at each end there was a stove and a hotplate connected by a horizontal flue to a central chimney. On the left-hand side of the flue there were gimcrack tables built up from basic wooden forms, and further forms on either side for seating. In this area, measuring 83 feet x 40 feet (about as long, but 7 foot wider than my Chigwell back garden) there were up to 250 prisoners, who had to live, cook, eat and sleep together in close proximity. The overcrowding and noise could be overwhelming, especially after curfew. Clothing and personal possessions had to be stored on the bunks. The bottom bunk occupant was lucky, as he had some space underneath for storage, and the top bunk occupant did not suffer from straw and dust falling from the straw-stuffed paillasse of the bunk above. The floors were like barn floors, with bricks set in earth. Lighting was supplied by four 25-watt bulbs. Daylight did not really penetrate the barracks, as many of the windows were broken and boarded up. There was a night latrine in the entrance – just a seat with a concrete cesspit underneath – which stank like hell, day and night. The wash and boiler house that divided the two barracks had large concrete troughs with several spray jets that had long since ceased to function. In any case, the water supply was sporadic, and it was even a problem to keep the boiler full for making communal brews during the day. Here, we washed our clothes when we could, and had our daily ablutions. Washes were often carried out with a 'Klim' tin of water. 'Klim', the reverse of the word 'milk', was the name of the Canadian milk powder that it had contained. It required great skill to get an adequate wash with that amount of water! The drainage system was poor, and leaked most of the time. As a result, there was a constant trickle of dank water down the main road that separated most of the huts.

After three weeks, the RAF contingent was transferred to the RAF compound, where about 2,000 (mostly aircrew) were housed. This compound was lockable, and when we got too boisterous, we were locked in as a punishment. Here, I met several chaps who were from 102 Squadron, or who had previously been with me at some time on the same training courses. Those from 102 Squadron wanted to know whether they had been reported as POWs. Of course, we didn't know, because 1943–44 was such a bad time for losses, and we had already been missing, and in Germany, by the time they would have been reported at home as POWs.

Our lives revolved around obtaining food and keeping warm. There is no doubt that these primary requirements of life are of paramount importance in a prison camp. Under the Geneva Convention, only basic provisions were supplied by Germany. We were not required to work (being officers or non-commissioned officers), thus food rations were the bare minimum and often of poor quality. The International Red Cross supplemented the needs of prisoners of war. Operating from Geneva, the Red Cross coordinated the supply of goods and distributed them to working parties, Stalags and Oflags, throughout Germany. The supply was mainly of food items, but clothing, books, musical instruments, and even correspondence courses for professional exams were organised for some camps. Supplies were often erratic, however, being governed by the prevailing war situation. Feeding POWs was obviously not the first priority in the German distribution system, especially as the war progressed, as the German transport infrastructure was gradually being destroyed by the RAF and the American Air Force.

The daily ration issued by the Germans consisted of about three boiled potatoes. These were often nearly rotten, after months of being stored in clamps. In addition, there was a ladle of watery soup called 'skilly'; this was made with turnips, swedes, millet, barley and dried sauerkraut or peas. The soup was issued at midday in 'skilly' buckets, from the cookhouse. There were two cookhouses, one British and the other French. The French cookhouse also catered for other nationalities. The pea soup was the most desirable 'skilly', and many rows broke out about how the small leftovers should be divided. Each barracks had an elected leader and two or three colleagues to assist him in making minor decisions, and sharing out any communal chores – and the pea soup share-out was one of his problems. In our barracks, after a vote by everybody, it was decided that the leftover soup should be shared out equally, pea by pea if necessary!

In the afternoon, a piece of black bread, about an inch or so thick, a small piece of margarine and a spoonful of beetroot jam, sugar or meat paste completed the hard rations. Several pails of ersatz coffee (made from roasted acorns) were usually put into the washhouse boiler for a hot drink later.

The Red Cross food parcel was based on the requirements of one person for a week. The parcels came from various countries: Britain, America, Canada, New Zealand, Argentina (for bulk rations) and sometimes France or Belgium. A British parcel contained a number of the following: a tin of condensed milk, 2 oz tea, a tin of cocoa, 4 oz sugar, 8 oz margarine, a tin of biscuits, 8 oz jam, marmalade or syrup, 2 oz processed cheese, a packet of dried fruit, or a tin of fruit pudding or creamed rice, rolled oats or oatmeal, a tin of meat and vegetables, a steak and kidney pudding or similar, a tin of sausages or meat roll, sometimes a tin of bacon or a Yorkshire pudding (instead of cocoa), a tin of egg powder, occasionally a carton of sweets, a 4 oz bar of chocolate, a tin of vegetables (peas, carrots etc), a tin of salmon or pilchards, a bar of soap, and perhaps a packet of salt, pepper or mustard. American parcels and some others contained cigarettes, but alternatively there was a separate issue of fifty cigarettes a week if whole parcels were issued. Otherwise, it was either twenty-five cigarettes a week or none at all, depending on the arrival, or non-arrival, of the parcels. Cigarettes were used throughout the camp as the main currency for trading and racketeering.

Together, the German ration and a full parcel every week was Utopia for us. Of course, there were weeks when we had only half parcels – or no parcels – or when distribution was disrupted for a variety of reasons. Consequently, tinned food had to be saved for hungry times. Most prisoners joined together in twos or more to share and prepare their food. The term for this was 'mucking in' and groups were called 'muckers'. John Bushell and I became 'muckers' and decided that we would prepare our food together every day.

On arrival we were given a dixie and spoon each, not much for preparing food, cooking, eating and drinking. We had to acquire knives, drinking cups and plates etc to begin with. We procured these by trading cigarettes with the 'Kriegies' (established prisoners of war). The Kriegies would have obtained the knives from the Russians, and the cups and plates would have been made from Red Cross tins by a Kriegie skilled in 'tin bashing'. Cups were Canadian 'Maple Leaf' butter tins with a handle made from a strip of tin attached to another strip, which was clamped to the top and bottom of the butter tin. Plates and dishes for heating or frying food were made from flattened-out Scotch biscuit tins turned up at the sides and with their corners folded in. Scotch biscuit tins were ideal for making all sorts of things; I don't know what we would have done without them!

The cooking stoves, one at each end of the barracks, were controlled by two stokers. The ovens were not used and only the hot plates were in action. Coal dust (compressed into briquettes) was used for cooking and was strictly rationed for each barracks. This meant that the stoves would only operate at lunchtime. The remainder of the briquettes were allocated to the washhouse, for use in the boiler for 'brewing up' during the day. Because the briquettes were rationed and were under the supervision of the guards, several attempts were made by various barracks to get more by false pretences. One barracks managed to obtain a spare set of keys to the briquette store. They cunningly organised a 'parade'. By marching with their familiar plywood Red Cross container, as if under the control of the guards, they obtained another issue of briquettes. But I don't think they managed it twice! Our barracks was luckier in this respect. There was a German Jew in our barracks, whose family had left Germany before the war. He had become a naturalised

British subject, had joined RAF ground crew, and had been posted to the Greek island of Kos. He became a POW after the Germans invaded the island in October 1943 and he was moved to Mühlberg. Naturally, he could speak fluent German and was able to approach two of the guards who, with their dogs, patrolled the camp after curfew. He bribed them with cigarettes to stay away on certain nights from patrolling the French cookhouse. This cookhouse, adjacent to our compound and opposite our barracks, had a large store of briquettes in the cellar, which could be accessed by cutting the barbed wire between our compound and the cookhouse. A group of volunteers in the barracks 'stood by' for these arrangements, and when the barracks leader announced, in true RAF parlance, 'Ops on tonight', there was great activity.

Prior to the first of these 'operations', the floor bricks had been removed from under one of the bunks. A pit had been dug and covered up with a false floor made of plywood from Red Cross packing cases. The removed floor bricks were then put back on top of the plywood, and earth was then spread in between the bricks. In the gloom of the barracks, it was almost impossible to detect any disturbance in the brick floor.

On 'ops' night, the pit was opened up, kit bags were borrowed, and, for half the night, kitbags full of briquettes that had been removed from the French cookhouse cellar, were unloaded almost silently into the pit. Well before daylight, the barbed wire was reconnected, the floor and bricks were replaced, and everyone involved was back in his bunk. The pit, which also housed other things that needed to be hidden, was never discovered, despite the many random searches that were carried out. This activity was undertaken every few weeks, and meant that we were both the most 'well provided for' barracks for cooking and the warmest in the whole camp, until the autumn of 1944.

Going back to cooking, the stokers maintained strict control over the hot plates, so that everyone had an opportunity to heat, boil or fry their food either in a tin, dixie or dish, by moving them in progression across the hottest part of the hot plate. Nevertheless, there were accidents, when dishes caught fire and tins exploded. When this happened, many of the contents, like creamed rice, hit the roof above! Sometimes food was cremated, as the hot plate suddenly went red hot in one spot. BRC bacon, when frying, could spit hot fat everywhere, and those nearest the stove had to dive for cover.

John and I, like most 'muckers', tried to add as much variety as possible to our meals. We would save barley soup for breakfast and convert it into porridge by adding sugar, or use it as a pudding at teatime, by adding dried fruit etc. Biscuits could be crumbled and mixed with various things. Sometimes our meagre and almost inedible bread ration would be mixed with fruit, meat or fish items to make a more acceptable bulk. Most of the 'skilly' soup items – turnip, swede or millet (bird seed) – we consumed straight away, especially if we were hungry. When a weekly full parcel arrived, most of the 'skilly' and some of the dry rations were given to the Russian amputees and, later, to the Italians.

Heating water for tea and coffee was difficult. The Army Kriegies from the Italian prison camps brought with them a design of a water heater called a 'blower'. It was a fan-operated device which, by means of a belt driving the fan at high speed, forced air into a firebox. The firebox was filled with anything burnable, such as pine cones, chips of wood and cardboard. By this means, a dixie of water that had been placed on top, would be boiling in a few minutes. 'Blowers' were made from Red Cross food tins and plywood, and were mounted on a bed board taken from a bunk. They were hazardous devices and so were confined to the wash-house. Unfortunately, the guards did not approve of these contraptions, and they frequently destroyed them. In a very short time, though, more were made, and then there were even fewer bed boards on some of the bunks!

A more organised way of providing hot drinks, an essential require-ment in cold, draughty and damp huts, was to use the boiler in the wash-house for communal brews. It was agreed that the issue of ersatz coffee would be reheated this way, and everybody would give up some of their tea, coffee and cocoa ration for regular hot drinks. The boilerman would shout out 'brew up' six or seven times a day and bodies would appear from bunks and out of nowhere with mugs and dixies to receive their ration.

Chapter 7

Daily Life as a POW

Every day at 6.30 a.m., the camp was awakened by guards running through the huts shouting 'Raus, raus!', and in double quick time we had to dress and form up in rows of 'fünf' (five), barracks by barracks in the compound. While the Army in their compounds, who were well disciplined, had their count finished in no time, the RAF were always late and virtually had to be driven out of their barracks. The guards regularly found stragglers still asleep in their bunks, or else they were not all lined up in fives. The German Unteroffizier in charge (a relatively young guard, who had been wounded on the Russian Front, and who was nicknamed 'Blondie', on account of his flaxen hair), was often at his wit's end with us. As a result of these events occurring day after day, Blondie would keep the offending barracks standing for hours in the slush and the snow. On one occasion, a member of another barracks brought out a chair for Blondie to sit on while this punishment was in progress, which he took in good part. But when, in another situation, he drew his pistol, it was time to call this game to an end!

Although roll call was always at 6.30 in the morning, curfew was later in the summer months, as late as 9.30 p.m., which made life much more pleasant, as it shortened the length of time during which we were incarcerated in the huts.

Not long after I reached the camp, and probably towards the end of that winter, typhus and diphtheria broke out, and the whole camp was quarantined. Typhus was to be expected at any time. It usually affected the Russians, because they were so weak, but it could break out anywhere. I can recall being bitten all over my body by bed bugs. Our paillasses were never replaced, and were pretty filthy sacks of straw. Living in such over-crowded conditions, lice, fleas and bedbugs abounded. This period was one of the most depressing times I can remember.

Quarantine meant that there was no roll call in the compound. No one was allowed outside the barracks for about a month, and this was enforced by having an armed guard posted outside each barracks entrance. Supplies were brought to the barracks and there was only the inside latrine to serve 200 or more of us, day and night.

When the camp was first built, a sewer system was planned, to take the sewage to the River Elbe some miles away. Camp reservoirs were dug to provide the water supply. This plan was soon abandoned, however, and latrines with concrete septic tanks were installed instead. Each barracks had an inside night latrine and, for each compound, one or more forty-seater day latrine buildings were added. Inside these there were four rows of boxed seats, each with ten holes, mounted above a large tank. No one felt alone in a forty-holer!

With more than 20,000 prisoners, the removal of the sewage was a permanent daily task for a small 'army' of the Russian Kommandos. Through a trap door on the ground outside the latrine, a long pipe, connected to a hand pump, was inserted into the decomposed sewage. With every operation of the pump lever, decomposed sewage was squirted into the hopper of a long wooden barrel, which was mounted on an ox-cart. The whole design could have been invented in medieval times, and was just as labour intensive as it would have been in those days. This operation generated the foulest stench, with every pump movement, and the ox-cart was christened 'the honey cart'.

Many honey carts were in action daily all over the camp. They leaked and left their signature everywhere, both inside the camp, and in a trail on their way out of the main gate to the local fields, where the sewage was used to fertilise the crops – including some of the inferior crops whose resulting vegetables we might consume in our 'skilly' in a few months' time!

The condition of the latrines and the inadequate method of sewage disposal for over 20,000 prisoners was beyond belief. The German nation, normally known for its discipline, thoroughness and cleanliness had, as

far as I was concerned, a blot on its character for the way in which it dealt
with prisoners of war in Stalag IVB – and probably in other camps as well.

There was no provision for toilet paper, and we had to resort to all
sorts of solutions! Red Cross tin labels were used for this purpose and,
sometimes, reading books had to be sacrificed. On one occasion, after a
Red Cross inspection, when we had complained about the lack of this
commodity, we did receive some 'toilet paper' from the Germans, in the
form of propaganda booklets printed in English. One was entitled *Jews
Must Live* and the other was *The Who's Who of Jews*. This listed all the
prominent people in the Western world and stated whether they were Jews
or not. The list included Churchill, who, of course, was not listed as a Jew.

Among over 7,500 British prisoners in the camp, there were many
talented people – and some who discovered hitherto hidden talents
during their time in captivity. Some lectured on their subjects in a small
hut set aside as a classroom; others were actors or musicians (mostly
amateur I believe), and they produced fantastic shows in a theatre and in
the barracks. And then there were the footballers, cricketers and rugby
players, who played on the pitches that were available in one or two compounds.

Unlike in other camps, there was no facility to study for professional
exams; mainly, I believe, because the British had come to the camp only
a few months beforehand, and there was no opportunity to set up a new
facility at this stage of the war. Also, the overcrowding in the barracks
made it impossible for serious study, due to the lack of space, the noise
of cooking, washing and general chatter etc. This was made worse in
the winter months because of the extended length of time we were herded
together between the curfew at night and the morning roll call.

However, I did manage to 'study' several subjects, mainly to keep my
mind occupied, on matters of interest to me. These were radio, intermediate maths, photography and psychology, for which classes were run.
The latter two classes closed down shortly afterwards, due to the removal
of the classroom, but that is another story! The lecturer on radio
communications, Robert Crawford, was an interesting person. I had first
met him when I was in the Army barracks. He had been a BBC engineer
in the Army, and his role was to assist a well-known BBC war reporter

named Ward. In those days, recording events for subsequent broad-casting, especially in front-line conditions, needed a qualified engineer to make the records. Ward and Crawford were captured in North Africa at Tobruk in June 1942. Crawford taught me a lot about basic radio, and was obviously quite involved in the (secret) construction of radios for the camp. There was always some route for getting supplies of essential parts! Crawford told me that they were worried that the camp might be overrun by the Russians, before the Western Allied forces could get there, and that we might need to be able to communicate with our Allies to obtain urgent assistance. To prepare for such an eventuality, the 'engineers' had built a transmitter, and had already selected a site for it. They had also acquired a starter motor from a Messerschmitt plane to generate the power for it. Fortunately, in the end, the transmitter was never used.

It was generally accepted that the camp theatre was a remarkable achievement. It provided first-class entertainment and raised morale for everyone in the camp. A spare barracks was found for the purpose. The brick floor was dug out and the bricks were replaced in tiers to provide the seating, so that the stage could be seen by everyone. A dimmer switch was even acquired for better control of the stage lighting.

The theatre group was in operation before I arrived at the camp and was now in full swing. With food parcels arriving more regularly, and the longer and warmer days of spring and summer ahead, our daily lives became more bearable in the dim, dismal, damp and dilapidated surroundings. The Second Front was expected soon, and with an early prospect to the end of the war, spirits were high. This was reflected in the energies of the theatre group, who produced both variety shows and straight plays, to great appreciation of their audiences.

My first visit to the 'theatre', aptly named the 'Empire', was only a few days after I arrived. The ticket was purchased with cigarettes, but I can't remember how many. It was a variety show entitled *Mühlberg Melodies of 1944*, a totally internally written production. The female impersonations were fantastic, impressing even the seasoned Kriegies, and especially me, a newcomer to camp life. The theatre props teams were wizards at making costumes from old blankets etc, and stage scenery and furniture from Red Cross boxes and plywood crates. Even the production of suits of armour was not beyond them! The 'tin bashers' got busy with Red Cross tins, and by clever lighting with green tinted bulbs, they were able to produce very realistic results.

The variety group produced several shows, some with leading camp comics, like *Music in the Cage, Let's Raes a Laugh, Knee-deep* and *Splash.* There were musical comedies such as *Springtime for Jennifer* with lyrics and music both written by the leader of the orchestra. The variety shows were alternated with straight plays presented by 'The Cads'. Each one seemed better than the previous production. Such productions were *Dover Road, The Man Who Came to Dinner, You Can't Take It With You* and *The Barretts of Wimpole Street.*

There were light classical orchestras and some who played more serious music. There were also dance- and swing-band performances. The latter groups also participated in shows in the barracks, providing suitable music. At leading football matches, boxing bouts, and on Sunday afternoons, a military band provided entertainment.

On some Sundays in the 'Empire', the Experimental Theatre Group presented some unusual plays based on melodrama, and those requiring 'audience participation'. One that I remember, called *Waiting for Lefty,* and which was about rebellious cab drivers, was highly successful. In this play, the audience, together with members of the cast (who, unbeknown to us, were 'planted' among the audience) got involved in a trade union strike. It resulted in the whole audience, quite spontaneously, standing up and shouting 'Strike, strike!' and 'Lefty', the ringleader being 'shot dead'!

Also on Sundays, church services were held in the theatre, and the padre (a New Zealander), organised entertainment and talks on some Sunday afternoons.

Another planned event for which the theatre was used was a remarkable exhibition of pendulum clocks! I presume that pendulum clocks were chosen because they operated by weights and not springs. All these clocks were constructed from flattened Red Cross food tins, which were cut into the various gears, cogs and other parts necessary to calibrate and display the correct time.

Hut shows were very popular and were introduced in the evenings in the summer months when the curfew was extended. Stage sets were erected from the hut seating and structures were brought in for the purpose. Such industry gave us all a feeling of involvement, and this added to the enjoyment of the entertainment that followed. Radio plays were very novel, being performed behind a curtain and in broadcasting style with all the sound effects. With the rest of the hut in semi-darkness (not difficult to achieve in a poorly lit hut) the right atmosphere was created for such plays as *The Tale of Two Cities*, *Ghost Train* and *Pygmalion*.

On other (winter) evenings, a series of talks were offered on such subjects as 'Big Game Hunting', 'The North West Frontier' and 'Russia'. These were given by prisoners with relevant personal experience. One talk, entitled 'HM Prisons', by a former prison warder, was an interesting one for us Kriegies! I also remember a talk by a former undertaker about some of his more gruesome experiences. We also had two demonstrations of hypnotism, one by a Dutch therapist who had practised in an Indonesian hospital, and another by a Kriegie who did it purely for entertainment and had us in fits of laughter by getting one of the audience under his 'influence', who knew nothing about the subject, to give us a talk on 'how to paint and decorate a room'. But the most impressive demonstration of all was when two fakirs from the Indian Army proved the results of self-hypnosis. They reduced their heartbeats until the point where, when cut, they did not bleed. Then they pinched two thick folds of skin over their stomachs and pierced them with spikes. When they pulled the spikes out, there was no trace of bleeding! Their second demonstration was even more amazing. They broke glass bottles on the floor, and when there was enough broken glass, one laid down on it on his back while the other stood momentarily on his chest. You could hear the crunch of glass under the first man's back! Again, when he got up, there was no trace of bleeding.

Another popular activity in the winter months was playing cards. This was mostly contract bridge, a game I learned as a POW. It became an obsession for some partners and was enjoyed almost without interruption, all day and sometimes into the night, with the participants only stopping to eat. This was possible with the larger groups of 'muckers', as cooking, chores, playing cards and other activities were shared out on a rota basis.

The most active and universal sport in the camp was soccer. Soccer was played throughout the day, all year round, but was most popular in the evenings during the summer months. I understand that the football equipment had been brought in from Italy by the Army POWs. Each hut had its own team, named after the 1st Division clubs in Britain of that era. Our hut's team was Blackburn Rovers, and the degree of interest in soccer was amazing. Our team had its own colours, and was well supported by the hut inmates. When we played in the 'League' matches, discussions were often very animated! I think the knock-out cup was the most exciting of all. Semi-finals and finals games were played on Saturday afternoons, and these became the main feature of the weekend. Newport County was by far the leading light in this competition and eventually won the cup. At Easter, Whitsun and on August bank holiday, there were gala matches, such as England v. Scotland, Army v. RAF, and Amateurs v. Professionals! The standard of play was very high indeed, and the teams, which were selected from several thousand possible players, gave a good account of themselves. Other feature matches were introduced, when a number of 'clubs' were formed from chaps who came from the same areas of the UK. Such examples were the 'London Club', the 'Heather Club', the 'Notts & Derby Club', the 'Kent Club', the 'Invicta Club' and the 'Lincolnshire Poachers'. All the clubs had badges, which had been made by the Russians out of aluminium dixies, and the clubs advertised their activities on wall posters. The Germans panicked when they saw the 'Lincolnshire Poachers' and issued a general warning that anyone caught poaching would risk being shot!

In addition to soccer, there was a Rugby League, and they played their important games on Sundays. Perhaps the most notable members of this league were the 'Springboks' and the 'Anzacs', and on many occasions blood was drawn when these two hefty teams met on the pitch!

During the cricket season, each hut entered a team, and the matches were played on similar lines to the soccer and rugby matches. The main feature of the cricket competition was a test match played between England and Australia or South Africa. This would take place over a weekend. Some of these were very close matches, on one occasion England beating Australia by just a few runs.

Two athletic meets were also held, and prior to these events, every morning and evening, contestants could be seen on the 'track' training with great zeal. The track was the perimeter of the football pitch, and it was an area that many Kriegies used to walk round every day for general exercise. Boxing was also a camp-organised sport, and as well as competitive bouts, exhibitions were sometimes carried out in a well-built ring in one of the compounds.

The Canadians were very keen on basketball and softball, while volleyball was undertaken by one and all. Others took up weight lifting and arranged physical training. Many of the competitive sports were played between the British and other nationals such as the French, Dutch, Russians and Poles; the latter two excelled at volleyball, and the former had a tough struggle when playing us at soccer – after all, it was our national game (in those days, in any case!).

There was no lack of exercise at Stalag IVB. The outdoor activity during the summer months, coupled with a good supply of Red Cross food parcels and encouraging news on the war front, kept us all in good spirits at that time. But of course all this was no real compensation for the abysmal living conditions and the lack of freedom we all experienced, especially for those who, like me, were only in their early twenties.

As previously mentioned, NCOs were not paid any service pay while in the prison camps. The Russian working parties were paid Lagermarks, but these were relatively worthless. There was a Russian canteen where items could be purchased, but there was nothing much to buy. However, items could be exchanged or bought and sold with cigarettes. Thus, cigarettes became the camp currency. There was an 'exchange rate', which fluctuated according to the amount of spare Red Cross food that was available, with how plentiful the Red Cross cigarettes were, and with the availability of any cigarettes that had been received in private parcels. In the summer of 1944, spare food was more abundant, and so the value of cigarettes as a currency fell, and in the winter of that year, with the reduction in the number of parcels that arrived, the position was reversed. The Russian canteen became the flea market (in more ways than one) where anything could be bought and sold or exchanged. The Italians, who arrived as prisoners with a complete kit of clothing and utensils, were seriously short of food, and were able to sell clothing, knives, scissors etc in return for basic food items. They even took on tailoring jobs in a trade-off for food and cigarettes. The Russians were in the best position to barter, because they were able to contact the farm workers in the fields and farms, and swap cigarettes and coffee for bread and any small items necessary for day to day living. They would conceal these items in their trousers, which was not very hygienic, especially when it was bread! I understand that the Russians who worked on the 'honey carts' were able to hide bread in the opening of the 'honey cart' barrels (when they were empty), on their way back to the camp – but you would need to be pretty desperate to eat this.

I recall a particularly memorable exchange that I witnessed one evening not long before curfew: a British chap had filled an empty cigarette packet with earth, except for ten cigarette stubs at the end, to represent a full packet. He then, in the half-light through the wire of the Russian compound, traded it for a long loaf of crusty bread. Back in the hut, he was full of his success in having duped the Russian. This was until he discovered that the side of the loaf had been sliced off, and that the whole of the inside had been hollowed out and filled with damp rags, to create the illusion that the loaf was of the correct weight. The side of the loaf had then been cleverly replaced with thin spills of wood to hold it in place. I often wonder who got the better deal. ...

On some evenings, the same RAF (German Jewish) POW who regularly 'organised' the coal stealing from the French cookhouse, would bring into the hut a patrolling German guard, complete with rifle. The guard would then stand in the middle of the hut and open the gasmask case that had been on his back, and which was now minus its gasmask. Inside, instead, he had toothbrushes, razors, razor blades, combs etc to barter for cigarettes, coffee and chocolate. Not every German soldier was waging war to the death!

I also remember a Dutch POW, who was still resplendent in his uniform with tassels and gold braid. The Dutch, until the Second Front, were well served with IRC food and parcels from home. This chap, like many Dutchmen, was very commercially minded, and he used to appear regularly in the huts carrying a large tray of goods that he was trading for cigarettes!

Planning to escape was naturally a very clandestine business, and unless you were personally involved, you didn't know much about it, as information was disseminated on a strictly 'need to know' basis, to minimise the risk of such information being leaked. However, there was an escape committee who would assist those who wished to 'have a go'.

There was one mass escape planned in the camp by the RAF, from the RAF compound. It was a very closely kept secret, only known to those involved. A hut used as a school for various classes was chosen as the site for the escape. This hut was without foundations and was raised up on blocks. Also, it was only a short distance from the camp boundary barbed wire on the northern side. The first move was to ask the Germans for permission for us to put a mound of earth around the perimeter of the hut 'to prevent footballs etc from being kicked underneath it'. A hatch was then cut into the floor of one of the classrooms, from which a tunnel was excavated to the outer wire. The earth dug out was packed tightly into the (now enclosed) space below the hut. As the distance from the hut to the field outside the wire was fairly short, the space was sufficient, and so the escapees did not need a complicated system to distribute the earth elsewhere. Also, concealment was less complicated, as classes were still being carried out in other schoolrooms, as before. I attended classes there, and I certainly did not know what was going on, and neither did the Germans! Bed boards were used to shore up the sides of the tunnel, and the hut wiring was 'tapped' to provide lighting for it. The bed boards would have been taken bit by bit from bunks in various barracks. As boards were already being consumed as firewood, or for blowers etc, it was accepted that this was part of the natural erosion of the camp. However, it did mean that for those who slept in the middle and lower bunks, more and more loops of paillasse were hanging down between the bed boards of the upper bunk.

The tunnel was completed in late summer, and the day before the planned night breakout disaster struck. A tractor towing a harvester, cropping the corn in the field beyond the wire, tipped into the tunnel exit, which was just below the level of the pasture. Immediately, all hell broke loose, as Feldwebel 'Piccolo Pete', our new German compound watch-dog, appeared on the scene. Piccolo Pete was a nasty, small, bow-legged fellow, who had taken over after Blondie had been posted elsewhere. He consistently made our lives a misery, making raids on our barracks without warning. He would appear with guards to block each end of the hut. We would then be searched and driven out immediately into the compound, while he and his posse of guards turned over the bunks and prodded the floor and everywhere else with picks, looking for signs of tunnels, escape material, blowers and radios etc.

Well, Piccolo Pete was in his element. The following morning, he turned up with the Russians and their cavalcade of honey carts, and they emptied the contents of our latrines and forty-holer, and poured it into the tunnel. Of course, classes were then closed at the hut and we never went near it again!

Another means of breaking out, usually through our own escape committee and sometimes with the help of the French escape committee, was achieved by exchanging identities with other prisoners who were on working parties. These were usually Army privates who, under the Geneva Convention, could be employed by the Germans in non-war-related industries. In the case of Stalag IVB, such employment would mostly be in farming. Additionally, new British POWs were often 'processed' through IVB, as it was also a registration camp, and one where new prisoners could be topped up with essential clothing. These prisoners would be approached by the escape committee and offered exchanges. They would have the benefit of not having to work, and the NCOs who changed places with them would have a chance to escape, which would be less risky than trying to flee from behind the wire at Stalag IVB. Both parties would, of course, lose their own identities during this time.

All those in our camp who decided to attempt an escape were given new identity papers, forged passes, travel documents, maps, and money etc. In my view, as a minimum they would have needed a good knowledge of German and the ability to live rough, as they would be hundreds of miles away from any territory where they could expect help from anyone. To my knowledge nearly all those in IVB who escaped were recaptured, brought back to the camp, and given fourteen days or more solitary confinement in the 'cooler' on basic rations. One chap who had done this and who had returned to the camp gave us a talk on his experiences. He told us that, having reached a railway siding, he found that none of the railway wagons were going to destinations on his chosen route, so he abandoned his plans. However, with a bit of quick thinking, he decided it would help the British war effort if he collected all the destination cards from the wagons, gave them a thorough shuffle, and then put them all back!

Geoff Taylor, who wrote the book *Piece of Cake* about prison life in Stalag IVB, tells his story about attempting an escape by stealing a Ju88 plane from Lonnewitz night-fighter training airfield near the camp. He and a colleague used the French and British escape committees to do an exchange with two French Arbeitskommandos. They got to the airfield and into a Ju88, only to be caught red-handed by a Luftwaffe guard! Luckily, they were wearing French uniforms and Geoff's colleague answered the challenge in French. The guard, thinking they were French farm workers from a nearby village, chastened them and told them to clear off, which they did at a rate of knots! After some time trying to find another aircraft that wasn't locked, and by then running out of food, they walked back into the camp and were hardly even challenged about where they had been.

After it became known that, on the orders of Hitler, fifty RAF evaders from Stalag Luft III had been shot in March 1944, the Germans gave out an official warning to all camps. It said that because of the increasing action of commando forces in Germany, many places were 'no go' areas, and that anyone entering them would be shot on sight. Escaping prisoners were therefore at an even greater risk of execution than previously. They were cautioned to remember that 'escaping was no longer a British sport'. The Stalag Luft III breakout was immortalised in the film *The Great Escape*, but of course was romanticised, so that the events of the film bore little relation to what had actually happened.

About the same time, a message was received from the British Government via the BBC news, which said that it was no longer the duty of prisoners of war to try to escape. I'm not sure that anyone would have attempted it out of a sense of duty – most would-be escapees had rather different motives.

We were allowed to write one letter and two postcards a month, so I had to ration them between family and friends over the fifteen months during which I was a prisoner. But I received 111 letters and about 6 or

7 parcels over that period. Everybody moaned in the hut every time my name and number (098 Wilson) was called out – 'What, not him again!' as I did receive a lot of post when compared with other inmates!

Letters to the UK and from Germany took about two and a half to three months each way, so a reply could take almost six months. The first letter I received after being shot down took five months, and the first letter from my parents took six months. Mail arrived fairly consistently after that, and I had received 43 letters by September 1944, 110 by January 1945, and then only one more before I was liberated in April 1945. Naturally, the progress of the war and the state of the infrastructure dictated the frequency with which mail was received, and it was pretty unpredictable.

My first parcel took seven months to reach me. It was from home, and contained 500 cigarettes – a fortune either as cigarettes or currency! My second and third contained books – fiction, biographies, a book on technical drawing, and – one on travel! My fourth parcel, also from home, contained clothing. Two previous parcels had been sent but these never arrived. These had contained cigarettes and, I believe, some chocolate.

I also received a parcel of books from the Red Cross, in which they had sent me two books that I had asked for, one on meteorology and the other on astronomy. I remember that I found the astronomy book fascinating. Stalag IVB, being located away from the town, in flat countryside and with no lights on late in the evening, presented an ideal situation for viewing the night sky, even through the few windows available. With my knowledge of the star constellations in the northern hemisphere, which I had acquired for astro-navigational purposes, I was able to identify the only star city outside our own galaxy that was visible to the naked eye – the nebula in Andromeda, near the constellation of Cassiopeia in the north-eastern sky. It gave me a great feeling of space and freedom and distracted my attention away from my dismal surroundings.

In my first letter home from Stalag IVB on 2 February 1944, I told my parents that our plane had caught fire and that I had had to bale out. (I did not say how or where, as this might have stopped the German censors from sending the letter on.) I also informed them that John Bushell was with me. We knew that Laurie Underwood and George Griffiths had survived, but there was no news of the others. I asked my family to send me underclothes, socks, toothpaste, cigarettes and photographs.

My letters started with mixed emotions. First and foremost, I was glad that I had survived and without injury. Also, at that time we were receiving weekly food parcels and the camp was providing entertainment with fairly frequent shows in the 'Empire' theatre. But the winter weather was miserable, with slush and mud everywhere, and with only lashed-up clogs to wear, there was no incentive to walk round the circuit of the 'football pitch'. Being incarcerated in these barracks during the long winter days was punishment indeed. Writing letters without receiving any in return became a burden, and it was not until I received my first letter in June did I brighten up. By then, the Second Front had commenced, the days were longer, sunny and warm, outside activities had started, and the parcels were still arriving weekly. As the D-Day invasion succeeded, a wave of optimism swept through the camp. 'Home by Christmas' was the cry! Of course, we were young Kriegies and did not realise that the older Kriegies had been uttering this same sentiment for the last three or four years already.

As the year advanced, France was liberated, Italy had capitulated, every-body was on a high, and our letters home reflected this mood. But the achievement of the Allied war on the ground and in the air across Europe was taking its toll on the German transport system, and our IRC food parcel deliveries started to become irregular. Setbacks, such as those at Arnhem in Holland, and the Battle of the Bulge in Belgium, ensured that the war would continue into the spring of 1945, and would worsen the conditions in the prison camp quite considerably.

In the autumn and winter of 1944, parcels were reduced by a half, and some weeks there were none at all. Coal for heating and cooking was cut back, and, as more prisoners came into the camp, it became excessively overcrowded. My letters did not mention this, and said our Christmas was fine, with an IRC parcel coming out of the blue, which enabled us to create some kind of festivities with 'concocted' mince pies (don't ask!) and Christmas pudding. Although we were able to organise a 'dance' for New Year's Day, we entered January 1945 facing the worst conditions that we had experienced so far in Stalag IVB.

News about the progress of the war was the very life blood of every prisoner. As the war drew to a close, events around us in the camp began to reflect the information we received.

We were lucky in IVB, inasmuch as the Army chaps had managed to bring their radios (in pieces) from Italy, concealed down their trousers, between their legs and anywhere else where they could hide them! The RAF had managed to bribe some of the guards for parts to assemble their own radio. So both compounds had radios, and were able to receive the BBC news every day. Despite random searches by Piccolo Pete and others, our radios were never discovered.

The news was taken down in shorthand and then transcribed, so that every barracks leader could read it out after the evening curfew. The leader would call for lookouts to make sure the outside was clear of roving patrols, and the hut would remain in complete silence while the bulletin was read out. Thus, throughout our time in IVB we were well informed about outside events, except on D-Day when the Germans told us first. That day, everyone went wild! Many were making crazy forecasts about the date when the war would end, and when it didn't, they were unceremoniously carried to the stagnant reservoir and thrown in.

About this time Italy capitulated, but the Germans continued to fight on in Italy. The Italian Army, overnight, became POWs, and several thousand of them arrived at the camp complete with all their kit. They were in a terrible state, as the Italians were despised by every nation. Italy had declared war on England when we were 'on our knees' after Dunkirk; thus they automatically became enemies of Russia and all the occupied nations. Now they were also the enemies of Germany. And the British Army POWs in IVB, who not long beforehand had been treated abysmally as POWs of the Italians, didn't think much of them either. So the Italians were soon starving, with poor rations, and were trading their kit for food, and begging alongside the Russian amputees for surplus 'skilly' and scraps.

In addition to the news we obtained from the radio, the Germans supplied us with a weekly newspaper called *The Camp*. I do not know how many they distributed, but I managed to keep three copies. These did not really supplement the BBC news, as they were a week or so out of date, and were really propaganda papers. Their war reports never mentioned Allied successes. They printed lots of bland articles taken from recent British newspapers, and the football league results. Their leader articles were loaded with propaganda. However the 30 July 1944 edition was interesting, as it covered the 20 July bomb plot to kill Hitler. It showed a picture of Hitler, apparently uninjured after the attempt on his life, talking to Mussolini. It announced 'that the plot by a criminal clique of German Officers had completely collapsed. The ringleaders either committed suicide after the outrage or were shot by battalions of the army. Amongst those executed was the manipulator of the explosive, Col. Count von Stauffenberg.' Incidently, he is now remembered as a hero by the German nation, and a street in Berlin is named after him: Stauffenbergstrasse.

This particular edition of *The Camp* also featured the launching of the V1 (flying bomb) weapons on London. The V1s were followed by the V2 rockets and these continued to be despatched from their launching sites in Holland and northern France almost until the end of the war. They were mostly aimed at the London area and at Antwerp (a major port for the British and Canadian Armies on the north European front). These weapons were totally indiscriminate, and some fell in Essex, many of them in the Ilford/Romford area where my parents resided. One V2 rocket nosedived into the road next to Joydon Drive, where my parents lived, and wiped out half-a-dozen houses and their occupants. Luckily, my parents and two sisters had evacuated to Brighton during this onslaught. But our house was damaged, and had to be patched up until after the war, when it was repaired. All this activity was unknown to me at the time, as my parents had not mentioned it, perhaps because they did not want to demoralise me any further.

There was heavy fighting in Normandy after D-Day and the German press made the most of it. At Caen, the first major city to be contested, the British and the Canadians suffered very heavy casualties, and the Americans on the Cherbourg Peninsular were held up for a time while capturing the port of Cherbourg. It was about five weeks before Caen fell, and by then the city had been almost demolished by Bomber Command. But the fighting drew in much of the German armour. At this time, the American forces made great headway in the Cherbourg Peninsular, and swept around Caen to Falaise, to form a pincer shape. The Germans, realising that they could be trapped, started to withdraw their tanks through what became known as the Falaise Gap. The RAF, with their rocket-firing Typhoon fighter bombers, had a field day destroying both troops and tanks. Eventually, the Germans discarded much of their equipment and went helter-skelter across the River Seine to avoid capture. By this time, the landing of Allied troops in southern France had taken place, and the Germans therefore decided to evacuate their troops from France.

The German 7thArmy was smashed at Falaise, with the loss of 250,000 troops, who were killed or captured, although a similar number managed to get away. Soon afterwards, an uprising took place in Paris, and the city was liberated by the French Second Armoured Division on 25 August 1944, almost without damage. By 3–4 September, the Allies had entered Belgium and Holland, and most of France was clear. In Stalag IVB, we followed all this news on BBC radio as it happened, and the camp was consequently in high spirits.

Now aerial activity was recommencing over Germany. (The bombing of Berlin, Leipzig and other cities during the winter months had been suspended, so that Bomber Command could assist with the securing of the Second Front. They were now released from this activity, and so night bombing began again.) Airfields were opened up in France, and fighter and fighter-bomber squadrons, both British and American, moved in to make use of them. American Mustangs were fitted with auxiliary fuel tanks, and were able to support the squadrons of their Flying Fortresses all the way to Berlin and further east. Now, in the height of summer, we were able to see these raids at 30–40,000 feet as hundreds of glinting specks in the sunlight and streaks of contrails in the sky. From now on, the Allied air forces controlled the sky. Both strategic and industrial German cities were bombed night and day and their roads and railways were under attack from dawn until dusk.

In August 1944, on the Eastern Front, the Russians were advancing on Warsaw. The Polish patriots, believing that the Russians would come to their aid, started an uprising in Warsaw. The patriots were not of the same 'political faith' as Stalin, and the Russian forces were ordered to hold off. Not only did the Russians stand back, they also refused to allow the RAF to refuel in Russian territory, and thus prevented them from dropping supplies to the Poles. The uprising lasted into September.

The German SS and the German Ukrainian Army perpetrated terrible atrocities in Warsaw, murdering thousands of civilians, including women and children. As they did so, they burnt their areas of the city to the ground. Eventually the whole city was virtually destroyed.

Sometime in late October or November, a long column of young Polish women and children from Warsaw reached our camp and were housed in the transit enclosure adjacent to the RAF compound. They were in a terrible condition. These young people, many of whom were boys of seven or eight years of age, or girls of sixteen years upwards, had been caught up in the patriot uprising, and had been serving as nurses and runners etc. Taken prisoner for their part in the uprising, they had been brought to Stalag IVB by cattle truck, or had simply been forced to march. They had no food or spare clothing and were desperate for help. The transit enclosure was filthy and dilapidated and had few latrines. It was almost unbelievable that the Germans could treat them as they did. Most of the nationalities in the camp spent a considerable amount of time standing along the wire between the compounds, looking at these young women, who, despite their condition, were cheerful, and sang Polish songs, often through the night. Of course, most prisoners had not encountered a female form for years, and to see so many at one time had awakened long forgotten aspirations! A number of the RAF prisoners were Polish, and there was a fair amount of communication with the women through the wire, almost to the level of romance. Although at the time we were getting short of food and had a limited amount of clothing, food and garments were given to these desperate Poles. After all this excitement, at roll call one morning we noticed that the adjacent compound was empty; the Polish women and children had disappeared. We had no idea what had happened to them. (In fact, it was not until January 1945 that the Russians took over the running of Poland, and occupied Warsaw in their advance towards Germany.)

After reaching the borders of Holland in September 1944, the Allies decided that a rapid crossing of the River Rhine into northern Germany would shorten the war by several months. It was planned to drop airborne troops to capture the Arnhem bridge across the Rhine in Holland, and hold it for a few days until armoured divisions from the south broke through. The 700 troops of the British 1st Airborne Division dropped by parachute into Arnhem. However, they were not, as had been planned, joined by those dropped at Oosterbeek, and were thus isolated at the northern end of the bridge. The armoured divisions from the south were not able to reach the bridge in time, and the 1st Airborne Division fought until they came to a standstill at Arnhem, having run out of ammunition. There were many casualties, and all those still alive were taken prisoner, together with those from Oosterbeek, who had been unable to get back across the Rhine. The 1st Airborne Division were regarded as heroes by the British and Germans alike. After several weeks of walking and travelling in cattle trucks, many arrived at Stalag IVB in an exhausted condition, but, nevertheless, they marched into the camp almost as if they were on parade. After a short stay for registration and other formalities, most were moved out, to join working parties else-where. The failure at Arnhem was a blow to our optimism about the hoped-for rapid end of the war, and we had to resign ourselves to the fact that we would have to see another Christmas through in 'Kriegieland'.

December 1944 arrived, and although Bomber Command had resumed its bombing deep into Germany, taking advantage of the long winter nights, not much had happened on the Western Front since Arnhem. Then, to everyone's surprise, General von Rundstedt's forces launched a massive strike into the American lines in the Ardennes on the 16th. The 106th American Infantry Division had just reached the area, directly from the USA, and had not been exposed to any action before. The Ardennes was a heavily forested region, now under snow, and the men of the 106th were probably thinking more about Christmas than a possible Blitzkrieg. The Germans took thousands of prisoners initially, made deep inroads into Belgium, and the port of Antwerp was threatened. It took some time for the Americans to halt the advance, and they were not helped by the bad weather, as to start with air strikes could not be carried out against the German armour. Eventually, the engagement known as the Battle of the Bulge, was won, at great cost to the Germans, who had run out of fuel. There were many prisoners on both sides. As a result, Stalag IVB was inundated with new American POWs. They arrived on Christmas Eve, and were the most dispirited group imaginable, suffering from dysentery and frostbite. They were starving, dirty, shivering, and exhausted. We had to sleep two or three to a bunk to accommodate the huge intake and, during the night, how we dealt with the men who had dysentery, with only one inside latrine, I cannot (or maybe do not wish to) remember. Luckily, as for food, there was an unexpected issue of IRC parcels, which to some extent 'saved the day' – it was Christmas after all!

I recall some interesting comments made to me at this time by some American prisoners. One said: 'Only three weeks ago I was in California, where I could eat as much chicken as I liked for a dollar.' Another complained that, when he had been taken prisoner, a German had frisked him and had taken sixty 'D Bars' (of chocolate) from him! Several said that some prisoners were mown down by a machine gun after they had surrendered. (It is recorded that there was a German SS atrocity, when some eighty-six Americans were shot, at around that time.)

The Americans were with us for about two weeks. Then they were moved out to various working parties, and our overcrowding returned to normal proportions. BBC news about the Western Front remained quiet, but we all brightened up when we learned about the Russians' sensational advance from the Vistula to the Oder Rivers. This was the only news that made life tolerable in January 1945, when we were suffering from extreme cold and damp in the barracks, and had very little food.

News for distribution was collated by budding journalists and artists. A weekly newspaper, designed like a normal broadsheet, with headlines, pictures and standard columns, was produced in manuscript. The pictures, portraits and cartoons were all hand drawn or painted. The pages were displayed side by side and affixed to a board made from a Red Cross crate, which was moved to a different barracks each day. The content would cover outdoor sports events, the 'Empire' theatre, and any topic of interest, including gossip! When the RAF came from Dulag Luft transit camp with a Red Cross issue of pyjamas, this made the headlines: 'RAF ARRIVE WITH PYJAMAS' – a great source of amusement for the Army POWs. A cartoon was published, showing an RAF chap coming down by parachute, after having been shot down, complete with his own Red Cross food parcel!

During the period 1943–45, the British were the most numerous of the POWs in the camp, but the French were the prisoners who had been there the longest (1939–45) and so were the best established of all the various nationalities. They had helped to build the camp in 1939, and were well entrenched with the Germans. (I suppose that, as the Germans were occupying their country, it was politic for them to be so).

The French ran the hospital and one of the cookhouses. They also did all the clerical work involved with keeping prisoners' records within the German administration, and they maintained the POW cemetery at Neuburxdorf, near Mühlberg. Over the years, they organised many religious parades. They had a good canteen, a university, and a theatre, which put on plays and musicals. But their greatest skill seemed to be in producing exhibitions and models. I saw two of their exhibitions – one entitled 'Paris' and the other called 'Mountaineering'. Their models were the last word in craftsmanship.

They lived well on the whole, getting black market food more easily than we could. Their connections were firmly established long before we arrived. They seemed to have a certain 'ownership' of Stalag IVB.

There were about sixty British deaths in the camp. Most of these were due to illnesses resulting from the unhygienic living conditions and an irregular supply of Red Cross food, as this was essential for maintaining reasonable health. However, three Britons were shot dead by guards, one committed suicide, and one died as the result of an accident. Of these:

- One was caught stealing coal at night.
- One was seen trying to pick wild strawberries from beyond the trip wire.
- One was caught at night, trying to return over the compound wire to his solitary confinement cell.
- The suicide hanged himself in the washhouse.
- The fatal accident was caused by a pilot from the nearby night-fighter training airfield at Lonnewitz. He 'shot up' the camp at low level, and hit two prisoners who were taking exercise by walking round the compound football pitch. One was killed and the other was seriously injured. The German pilot was subsequently court-martialled.

All these men had military funerals and were buried in a separate part of the Neuburxdorf cemetery. After the war they were reinterred in the 1939–45 Berlin War Cemetery.

Chapter 8

My Time Ends in Stalag IVB

At the end of January 1945, the Germans, having received confirmation of my commission from the Air Ministry, arranged for my transfer to Oflag VIIB in Bavaria. I knew from the letters I had received from home that I had been commissioned over a year before this, on 1 December 1943, and was now a Flying Officer, having been promoted automatically after six months. I was surprised that the Germans bothered to arrange this transfer, as the war could not last much longer. I had assumed that the move would be to Stalag Luft III in Poland, but I did not know then that the Russian advance had already forced the Germans to evacuate the whole of Luft III and march the POWs westwards.

I was sorry that I would have to leave behind Johnny Bushell, my 'mucker', as we had been good friends throughout my period at IVB, but I knew that he was the sociable type who would join another group after I had left. We agreed that we would have a grand party for 'us survivors' after the war.

The inmates of Stalag IVB had a hard time after I left, with few Red Cross parcels arriving, German rations cut and little fuel for heating. The theatre had closed down, and no doubt the outside activities were curtailed during the winter period. I believe that it was because of these conditions that John contracted tuberculosis after the war. In the last few weeks at the camp, there had been much aerial activity at low level from American Mustang aircraft, who were shooting at everything, including POW wood-collecting parties in the forest nearby. Because of this, the Germans agreed to have 'POW' painted on some of the roofs of the barracks to alert the Americans just who was underneath their guns!

On 23 April 1945, Russian Cossacks on horses, brandishing pistols and cutlasses, galloped down the main road of the camp, their tanks ripping through the barbed wire. Liberation day had arrived! The German guards, their families and some Polish POWs (who were no friends of the Russians) had evacuated the camp in buses the day before. I think that the Russians caught up with them, and they then faced the consequences of being over-run by an advancing army. …

The Russians occupied the German barracks and the administration area, from which the noise of drunken parties could apparently be heard for days. I understand that everything was chaotic in the camp – water and power supplies stopped, latrines remained unemptied, and there was no food distribution. Everybody had to forage for food and other supplies from the farms around, where many of the terrified German civilians were either dead (having been killed or committed suicide) or were still hiding in their cellars.

Eventually, the Russians organised a column to evacuate the camp to Reisa, by crossing the River Elbe at Strehla. This involved travelling along-side a long column of German refugees and liberated forced labourers, who were now displaced persons, heading west.

In Reisa, the Russians tried to register all the British ex-POWs. The Russians refused, with a display of arms, to allow some American troops with trucks to evacuate the British across the River Mulde (which the advancing American Army had reached). The British were now, in effect, prisoners of the Russians while they tried to trade them for Russian POWs released by the Americans. As a result of the general chaos that had developed since the camp had been liberated, many of the British (including Johnny Bushell and his friends) had made a run for it, steal-ing bicycles and carts and anything else they could find, in a move to get across a collapsed railway bridge over the River Mulde. The Americans were waiting on the other side with trucks to take them to Leipzig. For many of the British who remained under the control of the Russians, repatriation took several weeks.

My account of the liberation of Stalag IVB was based upon the accounts of other prisoners who remained there. For my part, as conditions at Stalag IVB had begun to deteriorate, on 2 February 1945, exactly one year after I had arrived, I had said goodbye to IVB with its 'not so pearly' gates and sinister black watchtower.

In a party of five RAF and RAAF (Royal Australian Air Force) chaps and three guards, we set out for Oflag VIIB, in Eichstätt, Bavaria. It was a harrowing time to be travelling on the German railways. The Russians, in their rapid push westwards, had caused a huge wave of movement of German refugees, all of whom were trying to escape from the advancing Russians by travelling to the west, having realised that the other Allies would be likely to treat them less harshly when the war ended. As a result, the railways were heavily congested. To make matters worse, the Allied air forces were bombing and strafing the roads and railways around the clock.

I had thought that travelling like a civilian, and not in the usual cattle trucks, would make it a reasonable journey, especially after having spent a year incarcerated in Stalag IVB, but I was wrong. The first train we caught from the nearby junction was very late, and literally crawled all the way to Chemnitz, where we lingered seven hours for our next connection. We were waiting for a train to Nuremberg on a platform crowded with refugees, all with bundles of clothing and luggage packs. Also, there were many hospital cases of wounded soldiers about, looking very sick; pale and thin specimens, all of them. Chemnitz was regarded as a hospital centre and had not yet been bombed. Up until this point, the railway junction had remained intact. The station was still selling refreshments (a watery beer), but had no bookstalls or buffet. The refugees had already waited hours for a train and now there was another delay of seventy minutes. They took it without a murmur and just moved back from the platform edge yet another time. I suppose they had given up. On the other hand, on the opposite track, military trains loaded with panzer troops were passing through, no doubt destined for the Eastern Front. I wondered where they would be in a few days' time.

We left Chemnitz, just ten days or so before the town was heavily bombed for the first time, alongside Dresden. Together with my four companions, I had certainly witnessed the strategic importance of Chemnitz as a busy rail junction for German armour. This ultimately made it a legitimate target for bombing, in a state of total war, in spite of its status as a hospital centre. I later learned that, at the Yalta Conference on 4 February 1945, the Allies – Churchill, Roosevelt and Stalin – had agreed to assist the Russian advance by bombing the important rail heads through which the German armour would pass to the Eastern Front. These rail heads were at Leipzig, Chemnitz and Dresden. Unfortunately, Dresden in particular suffered a very high loss of life as a result of the heavy bombing and the firestorm that subsequently developed, due to the existence of the many medieval buildings in the town, which were primarily built from timber.

After leaving Chemnitz, we continued southwards at a very slow pace, and eventually reached Plauen. We arrived at midnight and our next train left at 5 a.m. Plauen station had been badly damaged by bombing and we had five hours of very draughty waiting. The civilians (refugees) were in the same position as us, and there was no shelter and no escape from the cold. Apparently, a youth movement of girls and boys of about ten years old and resident in the town, had been recruited to assist these people in their plight, by helping with their baggage or aiding them in other ways. It was clear that a sense of emergency was developing as the Russians closed in on the German homeland, and the Germans were resorting to desperate measures to help their war effort. But what drudgery, and to what avail? The situation seemed hopeless.

Hof was our next port of call. We got there at about 9.30 a.m., and as there was another long wait, our guards managed to get us into a hut with a stove in it, on which we were able to brew some coffee to drink with our bread. This made all the difference, and we felt alive again. It was about 5.00 p.m. that day before we moved on. The train was packed, as more and more people were on the move, all having endured many hours of waiting for connections. It was clear that the railways were in complete disarray. The continuous bombing had made its mark and we were lucky that we had not been bombed ourselves so far. We had a quick change of trains at 7.00 p.m., but what a carriage we had! The train had been strafed; it had no windows at all, and we froze all the way to Nuremberg, which we did not reach until midnight. Here the maelstrom of refugees continued to swell, and the station was almost in darkness. We were led virtually by the nose to an air-raid shelter. It was an excellent shelter, with air conditioning, and plenty of warmth. Whether there was an air-raid or not I do not know, but it was a joy to thaw out. It was another six hours before we moved on again.

I did not record the details of the remainder of my journey, but Oflag VIIB was about 50 miles further south, only a few miles north of the Danube.

We arrived at Oflag VIIB on 4 or 5 February 1945. The camp was situated in a small valley running east–west. About a mile away to the south was a road stretching parallel to the camp. Beyond the road were hills forested with pines and other trees. On the north side was another road, running alongside the camp. Rising from this was a craggy area, with pine trees scattered along its ridge. It was a very pretty location. What a contrast to Stalag IVB, which had seemed like Siberia on my arrival there, almost exactly a year beforehand.

The camp housed about 1,500 officer POWs, all Army personnel, from the British Commonwealth. Now there were five RAF and RAAF POWs too! It was not like Stalag IVB, which had over 20,000 POWs from many nations. The camp was divided into two sections, called Upper and Lower camps, separated by a football pitch and an ice hockey ground, which had been laid out by the prisoners themselves. The Upper camp was a pre-war-built set of barracks, with good sanitation and stoves in each room. The Lower camp was made up of five wooden huts with separate room areas and brick stoves, but the sanitation was not as good as in the Upper section. Nevertheless, the whole camp was like a five-star hotel compared with Stalag IVB. Tom Nelson (also an RAF navigator) and I were in the Lower camp, but whenever possible, we used the normal private flush toilets of the Upper camp. I can remember that I used to make special journeys to these toilets to enjoy the delights of being in a situation that was just like home!

We were boarded in a hut with a portion divided off as a room. We had two sets of double bunks, a tall cupboard on its side that served as a sideboard, with the top as a work surface and storage underneath. There were two easy chairs and a table made from Red Cross crates, and we used the services of a communal stove for cooking. The stove was a Kriegie modification set into the chimney of the main stove, made up of RC tins and a German pickle tin as a firebox. It enabled us to brew up tea and other hot drinks, and to heat up food and keep it warm. The fuel was mostly pine cones (gathered by the wood-collecting parties) kept alight by a forced draught, which was generated by waving a table tennis bat into the opening of the 'firebox'. I have often wondered whether the design could have been patented!

Tom and I were allocated a room with two Australians (Jack Bedells and Nigel Teague) as a mess of four. Jack seemed to be in charge of the German and Red Cross food rations. He also organised a weekly menu and cooked the meals most of the time. In Army parlance he was President of the Mess Committee, or PMC – gone were the Stalag days of 'muckers'. I cannot recall making any meals but I did a lot of washing up! Although Jack prepared most of the meals, he was a bit of a hoarder. When, from time to time, Jack was out on wood-collecting parties, Nigel (Paddy) would take over and have a bit of a bash. On one occasion, he used up all the chocolate from our RC parcels, which he melted down with some margarine, and mixed with a tin of biscuits and solid oatmeal (all crushed up), and some Bengers food and egg powder. When it had set, it became a delicious fudge-like substance. A bit expensive, but by this time it was Easter and the news from the outside world was good, so we had a celebration. Another time, Jack had tried his hand at making cakes but had used salt instead of sugar. As cakes, they were a disaster, but used with a tin of stewed steak, they became acceptable Yorkshire puddings!

Jack, and Paddy (a man of few words), had obviously elected to look after us and they were very friendly chaps, but we found that they were very quiet, and to some extent introspective. In fact, most of the people at this new camp were like that, and I can only draw the conclusion that they had 'run out of steam'. They had all been prisoners for four or five years, had seen the same number of Christmases go by, and were still behind the wire. Now that the war was almost over, they were just waiting for it to end, and had no other horizons. However, there were still some activities in the camp at this time, and I can recall going to the theatre to listen to a recital of Gilbert and Sullivan music. Looking at some of their old programmes and magazines, I could see that it had been a lively place at one time. These prisoners were in the privileged position of having all their 'literature' printed. I suppose that, as they received some of their UK pay in Lagermarks, they could pay for this work to be done outside the camp. (I cannot recall whether I was receiving any pay at this time; anyway it was too late by this time to bother about enquiring about such things.)

On the road to the south, nearly every day, and in the distance, we could see a troop of Germans marching up and down as if in training, and singing as they marched. We called them 'the singing Goons'. (Germans were often nicknamed Jerries, Krauts, or Goons.) I believe they were the Volkssturm – the German 'Homeguard'– which was made up of a combination of members of the Hitler Youth and old men. It was a question of 'all hands on deck'. The members of the Volkssturm had been recruited to defend the homeland now that it was being invaded on all fronts. In January 1945, Hitler ordered that, to strengthen their resolve, the Volkssturm would be regrouped with regular Army units. In the Russian battle for Berlin in April of that year, many of them were serving alongside the more seasoned regular troops, in spite of their age (very young or very old) and lack of experience or training, and many were subsequently killed.

Another event that comes to mind of this late hour of the war occurred when we had our paillasses removed as a punishment for some misdemeanour that the Allies had allegedly committed against the Germans. We had to sleep on bare boards for about a month, and this was not kind to our hips, which by this time didn't have much flesh left on them.

On 12 April 1945, the Germans informed us that President Roosevelt had died, which was not really a surprise as he had been ill for a long time. (It was a pity that he did not live to see victory, which was less than a month away.) We all assembled as for roll call, and had two minutes' silence as a mark of respect for him.

On 9 March I received a blank book issued by the International Red Cross, named 'A Wartime Log'. It contained pages that could be used as a diary (a bit late in the day for that!) or just to record anything; the centre pages were for sketching etc and there was a rear section with cellophane envelopes designed to store small items. I spent some time catching up, by writing as much as I could remember of the last year's events, and I drew pictures of my present camp and other points of interest. I also affixed photographs that I had received from home. Unfortunately, I was unable to complete the diary, but it has supplied a substantial part of the material for this account of my POW days. I was extremely grateful to receive the diary, as otherwise this account would never have been written!

From February through to April, in common with the prisoners in Stalag IVB, we did not have many Red Cross parcels. One week we were lucky, as a truck was diverted through to us, so it was a kind of 'rags to riches' situation, with weeks of plenty followed by weeks of nothing. On 9 March we were told that the German rations were being cut by 20% and the potato ration by 33.3%. German rations were poor, but were more necessary than ever to us as the supply of Red Cross parcels was dwindling. We were hoping fervently that the war would be over soon.

There was rapid progress in the success of the Allied war from February onwards. The Allies fought through the Siegfried Line in Germany to the Rhine, and took Cologne on 6 March. Then, the only surviving bridge over the Rhine at Remagen was captured. From 23 to 26 March, the American armies in the Ruhr area crossed that part of the Rhine, and the British and Canadian airborne and ground troops in the north passed over the Rhine near Wesel, in the greatest operation since D-Day. More than sixty bridgeheads were established. As a result, massive advances were made. The British and Canadian forces traversed northern Germany in seven days and reached the Baltic. The American armies had encircled the Ruhr and moved east to central and southern Germany.

These events really were the beginning of the end of our war. On 13 April, we were informed by the commandant that the camp was to be evacuated the next day to Stalag VIIA, at Moosburg, some 60 miles or so south, across the River Danube. We would march there, with a truck to take any of us who were unable to walk the whole distance. Considering the rate of the American advance under General Patton, it beggars belief that it was considered worth the effort to move us at all. I understand that it had been a standing order from Hitler that no prisoner should fall into 'enemy' hands – but this was now quite irrelevant, as he was rapidly losing the war.

Chapter 9

On the Move Again!

The date of 13 April was a hectic day for everybody. We had to gather up as much food as possible – luckily there had been a Red Cross parcel delivery that week. We also had to pack essential clothing and other personal items into kitbags and home-made rucksacks. Some POWs had procured old prams and others had attached makeshift wheels to Canadian Red Cross crates to lessen their load! A number of us had managed to get hold of poles, so that two kitbags could be suspended between the shoulders of two people.

It was a motley army of men who assembled on the road just outside the camp the following day. At about 9.30 a.m., some 1,500 Kriegies, in a very long column interspersed with German guards, were ready to move off. Then, low over the horizon from the east, there swept in a flight of fighter aircraft. The Army chap next to me said, 'What are they?' and I replied, 'They look like Me109s.' How wrong could one be? In seconds, the planes had shot at, and straddled with light bombs, a German truck that was on the road to the south of us. This was a flight of American Mustang fighter-bombers! Now it was our turn; the Mustangs wheeled around and, flying in again from the east, started to strafe our column. Pandemonium broke out as the column scattered off the road. Fortunately, I was in the middle of the column and managed to sprint off the road in time, before the cannon shells started to spurt along it. Those at the front of the column weren't so lucky. Then, either the aircraft wheeled around again, or another flight appeared in the same run. By this time, I was trying to run up the hill to a craggy outcrop for shelter. The Mustangs were flying at barely 50 feet and were firing their cannon. My legs just folded up under me in fright and I didn't make it to the shelter of the

Reg as a new recruit. 1941.
(Wilson family)

**Reg at Niagara Falls in June 1942, during his
training in the USA and Canada.** *(Wilson family)*

Course 53, with Reg seated in the front row, third from the right, 1941. *(Wilson family)*

Pilot George Griffiths.
(Griffiths family)

Second dickey pilot Kenneth Stanbridge.
(Stanbridge family)

Bomb aimer Laurie Underwood.
(Underwood family)

Flight engineer John Bremner.
(Bremner family)

Wireless operator Eric Church.
(Church family)

Rear gunner John Bushell.
(Bushell family)

A Halifax of No. 10 Squadron in December 1942.*(MOD)*

Reg Wilson with his Halifax bomber in the back-
ground, 1942. *(Wilson family)*

'Facing the Music'. Acrylic painting depicting the
fateful last flight of Halifax LW337. *(Kai Choi,
aviation artist and friend of the Wilson family)*

THE LAST FLIGHT OF "OLD FLO" BERLIN 20th JAN '44.

Sketch in Reg's POW logbook depicting 'The Last Flight of Old Flo'. *(Wilson family)*

The dreaded 'Regret to inform you …' telegram. *(Wilson family)*

54, Everglen Grove,
Durham.

Newcastle upon Tyne. Feb. 14th
1944

Dear Mrs. Wilson,

I feel that I would like you to know of the sympathy which I and my family feel for you during the very anxious & trying time which lies ahead for all of us whose sons were members of the crew of which my son, Jack, was Flight Engineer.

It is very hard to look on the bright side at a time like this, and I appreciate fully that this letter, though very sincere, will not help you to bear the great sorrow which all of us must surely feel.

I would, however, like you to know that my thoughts are with you during this period of waiting - and I hope that soon our minds will be at rest through our receiving good news either from our sons themselves or from the Air Ministry.

Ada Bremner's letter to May Wilson, written while their boys were still unaccounted for (see following page for continuation of this letter). *(Wilson family)*

Should you receive news of the whereabouts of your boy, would you be so kind as to inform me. I would be most grateful. In the meantime let us hope that all is well with each one of them.

I am.

Yours Very Sincerely.

Ida . Blemner .

POST OFFICE

TELEGRAM

No.

ROMFORD OFFICE STAMP 10 MR 44 ESSEX

ees to pay   d.

RECEIVED

Prefix.   Time handed in.   Office of Origin and Service Instructions.   Words.

73/20

From

6.18   LONDON TELEX OHMS   PTY CC 54

(PRIORITY CC) W J WILSON ESQ   28 JOYDON DRIVE

CHADWELL HEATH ROMFORD ESSEX =

FROM AIR MINISTRY 77 OXFORD ST W 1   PC 280

10/3/44 INFORMATION RECEIVED THROUGH THE

INTERNATIONAL RED CROSS COMMITTEE STATES THAT

YOUR SON P/O REGINALD CHARLES WILSON IS A PRISONER

OF WAR IN GERMAN HANDS. STOP LETTER CONFIRMING
THIS TELEGRAM FOLLOWS. STOP = 1544 A + +

+ 28 JOYDON DRIVE ++   W 1 ONE   PC 28C ONE
10/3/44   1544 A ONE + + +

Left and this page, top:
Confirmation that Reg was a POW.
A huge relief when compared with
the alternative. ...

Above: Family pictures in Reg's
POW logbook. Left to right: May
and William Wilson (parents) and
sisters May, Doris and Vera.

Right: Reg's Stalag IVB POW
identity tag.
(All images: Wilson family)

Kriegsgefangenenlager Datum 27-1-44.

MY DEAR MUM + DAD, I AM NOW
IN GERMANY. YOU CANNOT WRITE UNTIL
I REACH A P.O.W. CAMP. PLEASE KEEP
IN TOUCH WITH RED CROSS. I AM
UNHURT AND QUITE WELL. PLEASE
TELL PAT I AM SAFE. MEANWHILE
DO NOT WORRY AT ALL.
ALL MY LOVE. REG.

Received 21.3.44 LUFT. POST.
AIR MAIL

Kriegsgefangenenpost

GEPRÜFT
Postkarte

Mit Luftpost
Par Avion

-2.2.44.0

PASSED
P.W. 5858
Gebührenfrei

An

MR + MRS WILSON
38, JOYDON DRIVE.
CHADWELL HEATH.
ROMFORD

Empfangsort:

Absender:

Vor- und Zuname:
F/SGT WILSON R.C.
RAF. 138940/.

Straße: ESSEX

Gefangenennummer:

Lager-Bezeichnung:
Dulag Luft

Land: ENGLAND
Landesteil (Provinz usw.)

Deutschland (Allemagne)

Reg's postcard telling his parents he was a POW. *(Wilson family)*

Reg's second POW camp (Oflag VIIB) as sketched in his logbook, spring 1945. *(Wilson family)*

Cooking the POW way in Oflag VIIB, where conditions were much better than in Stalag IVB, spring 1945. *(Wilson family)*

The superior living conditions in Oflag VIIB! Spring 1945. *(Wilson family)*

A farmyard in Bavaria, sketched during the futile march away from the rapidly advancing liberating forces, April 1945. *(Wilson family)*

Reunion of the four survivors at Laurie Underwood's wedding in June 1945. Men, from left: Reg Wilson, George Griffiths, Laurie Underwood (groom) and John Bushell. *(Wilson family)*

A reunion on Laurie Underwood's golden wedding anniversary in June 1995. From left to right are George Griffiths, Laurie Underwood, Reg Wilson, John Bushell. *(Wilson family)*

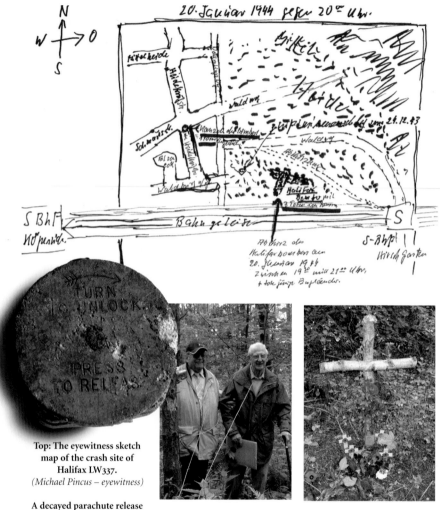

Top: The eyewitness sketch
map of the crash site of
Halifax LW337.
(Michael Pincus – eyewitness)

A decayed parachute release
found with the remains of
John Bremner. *(Ralf Drescher)*

**Eyewitness Michael Pincus and Reg 'arm in arm' at the crash site in
May 2006** *(Wilson family)* **Crash site.** *(Ralf Drescher)*

Above and opposite page, top: the piece of wreckage which identified Halifax LW337. *(Ralf Drescher)*

The pivotal moment – eyewitness Michael Pincus shows his schoolboy diary entry to members of the Wilson and Hughes families, October 2005. *(Werner Zimmermann)*

At the British Embassy in Berlin. Left to right: Barbara Wilson, Hazel Griffiths (pilot's widow), Marjorie Acon (John Bremner's sister), Reg Wilson, John Bushell (rear gunner), Michael Church (son of wireless operator), Bernice de Heaume (daughter of Ken Stanbridge, Second dickey pilot). *(Wilson family)*

Above, left: A happy reunion – Reg (seated) with (from left to right) wife Barbara, David and Janet Hughes, Ralf Drescher, Stefan Salem (Fellerer's grandson) and Stefan's girlfriend. Above, right: Reg with journalist Ralf Drescher on Reg's ninetieth birthday – 26 January 2013. *(Wilson family)*

Above, left: Marjorie and John Bremner at home in Newcastle during their childhood. *(Bremner family)*
Above, right: Marjorie Acon (née Bremner) in October 2008 at the British Embassy in Berlin.
(Wilson family)

John Bremner's funeral in Berlin, 16 October 2008 *(Wilson family)*

Reg Wilson lays a wreath at the grave of his fellow airman John Bremner. *(Wilson family)*

Above, left: Author Janet Hughes at the grave of John Bremner. Above, right: The headstone which now marks the resting place of John Bremner. *(Wilson family)*

Left: Reg and Barbara Wilson with their children and grandchildren on the occasion of Reg's ninetieth birthday, 26 January 2013. *(Wilson family)*

Below: Reg Wilson at John Bremner's burial ceremony. *(Wilson family)*

rock. I have never felt so vulnerable, before or since. The Mustangs on this pass were, I believe, firing at a machine-gun post on the top of the ridge. They apparently ran out of ammunition then, as after this they disappeared.

The results of this strafing were tragic: there were some fifty casualties, including seven who were killed and another three who died of their injuries within twelve hours. The leader of the camp dance band, who was a first-class pianist, lost an arm, and another man had to have a leg amputated. These events were even more devastating when one considers that these chaps had been prisoners for four or five years and were within two weeks of being liberated. We all moved back into the camp, and the letters 'POW' were marked out on the football field. It was decided by the commandant – who had had two of his guards killed and several more wounded – that the evacuation would recommence the next evening. We would march by night and lie up under cover during the day. Nobody disagreed with that decision.

Some days after we had left the camp, the American Army arrived and repatriated the wounded. The event was serious enough for a question to be asked in the House of Commons as to why a motley column of POWs, in khaki, and just outside the wire of their camp with its watch-towers and searchlights, could be mistaken for a disciplined column of the German Army. The reply was that the American Air Force thought that we were a troop of Hungarians, whose uniforms were also coloured khaki. This was an example of the suffering caused by so-called 'friendly fire', of which there were a number of incidents in the Second World War.

The march to Stalag VIIA took about six or seven nights and, unfortunately, I did not record any details of it. There were no further serious incidents during the march and, since it was taking place at night, not much could be seen. It was more of a trudge along than a march. As there were no real main roads, it was quiet, and there were no German troops or armour moving north and no hoards of refugees moving south. There were no towns and we only passed through a few villages. I don't recall crossing the Danube, but this would have been a natural defence for the Germans as the Americans advanced south. I understand that pockets of SS troops were active in the forests around Eichstätt, but we did not see or hear any as we moved south.

In my wartime log, I did make a sketch of an open barn and farmyard that typified the sort of place we stayed in after each night's march. These farms would have been spread around a village, and we were allowed to wander anywhere on parole status. This meant that we would not try to escape. Not that there was any point in escaping at this stage of the war, with the risk of being caught up in a local SS firefight and with the war being almost over. Some of the chaps did roam around the farms and houses, trading with locals their cigarettes for such foodstuffs as bread and eggs. On one occasion, I went into a local church and I found a memorial card for a German soldier who was killed in 1941, 'gefallen für Deutschland', and which I kept as a reminder that, in such a war, the youth of every nation is sacrificed. It makes little difference to those whom they leave behind whether or not they died for a just cause, as the grief experienced by those who survive them is just as acute in either case, and should never be underestimated.

One event I do remember clearly occurred in the fading daylight as we moved off one evening. I saw two old men just completing a new ornamental wooden fence around their front garden. Each pale of the fence had a cloverleaf-shaped hole carefully cut into it at the top with a bow saw. The two old men were so immersed in their work that they didn't notice us as we passed by. Even though much of Germany was in turmoil, the war could have been a thousand miles away, or might never even have happened, as far as they were concerned. They were just getting on with their lives.

On 22 April, we reached Stalag VIIA, and it was nearly the end of the war.

The building of Stalag VIIA in Moosburg, Bavaria, was started in September 1939. The camp was designed for 10,000 POWs and grew to an enormous size over the war years. After the collapse of France, the evacuation at Dunkirk, and the invasion of Russia in 1941, prisoners from seventy-two nations had passed through the camp. Towards the end of the war, there were about 80,000 POWs and 2,000 guards and administrative staff, with another 80,000 prisoners and 8,000 guards on the outside in working parties. No doubt these numbers had been swollen by the intake of prisoners from other camps likely to be overrun by the Russians, such as ours. In the final stages, the commandant had requisitioned tents for 30,000 of the prisoners, but we were housed in huts when we arrived.

The huts were like those in Stalag IVB, but were probably even more dilapidated, if that were possible, and the whole place was flea-ridden. This would have been a terrible shock for our colleagues from Oflag VIIB, who had had tolerable living conditions for some years. However, in the event, we only had to suffer there for a week until our liberation.

On the morning of 29 April we assembled for roll call. However, we found there were no guards to count us and no guards in the watchtowers! Then we heard the rumble of trucks and tanks getting steadily nearer the camp and then passing by, a little way away, but we could not see them. There were a few light explosions and some small-arms fire as the column approached the town. This stopped, and in the distance we could see the American flag, the Stars and Stripes, go up over the town hall. Our war was over! What a 'Hollywood ending' for us to experience!

Shortly afterwards, an American jeep from General Patton's 3rd Army entered the camp. In it, a soldier was standing up, holding aloft the commandant's revolver, which had just been surrendered to him. You couldn't see the rest of the jeep for people trying to climb on to it. The camp was now in a state of total euphoria!

I have since learned that Colonel Burger, the German officer responsible for the defence of Moosburg, wanted to hand over the camp to the advancing Americans and for the Americans to bypass the town. By this means, he would ensure the safety of the camp and the town. However, Colonel Burger had received orders to deport all the 15,000 POW officers in the camp, and to send as many of his own men as he could afford to defend Moosburg. The local command of Moosburg was then taken over on 28 April by an officer of the SS, who was tricked into believing that Burger was going to carry out the deportation orders. When the SS officer had left, Burger informed the more senior POW officers, in the presence of the commandant, of his decision to hand over the camp en bloc to the approaching Americans. On the night of 28 April, under a flag of truce, a delegation – including a Swiss representative, two

POW colonels and the SS officer – contacted the Americans to persuade them to go round Moosburg. The Americans held on to the SS officer (as Burger knew they would), and declined to go round Moosburg, but accepted the plan to take over the camp from noon on 29 April. This was carried out with only token resistance in Moosburg (as I actually witnessed) and there were no casualties during the American take over of the camp. (I have often thought, since, that the reason the German SS wished to hold on to as many officer prisoners as possible, was to use them as hostages to trade for their own lives when the end came.)

Now that we had been liberated, all we wanted to do was to catch a plane home. But the repatriation of so many men was a prodigious task, and it was obvious that a considerable amount of organisation would be necessary before this could happen. The first thing I can remember was that a number of American ladies, who were assisting the Red Cross, appeared, all highly made up, as if they were going to a party. They were distributing doughnuts and white bread, which after eating the German bread for fifteen months, tasted like cake! It was a nice gesture, but I think that what we would have appreciated more, was a field kitchen with some thick soup and US Army rations!

The Americans were concerned that in such a large camp, with so many nationalities, discipline would weaken, and that the inmates would break out and ravage the town. So we, the British officers, were required to patrol on the outside of the wire, in pairs, in the hope that we could maintain order. We had no weapons, but luckily no break-outs materialised. I was very relieved when they withdrew this requirement, as we could not really have prevented any trouble and, instead, we might have ended up as post-war casualties.

Plans to evacuate us unfolded fairly rapidly, and I was scheduled to fly to Brussels on 3 May, but this flight was cancelled. On 6 May, I wrote an American air letter home, a rather sad letter as now I was disappointed about the delay, and conditions in the camp were terrible. I am glad to say that this letter didn't arrive home until I had already been there for several weeks!

Eventually a number of us were moved on 8 May to a grass airfield adjacent to Moosburg town, where some forty American Dakota transport aircraft were due to land to take us to Brussels. None arrived, however, and we spent all day in glorious sunshine on the airfield, which meant we would all reach home sunburnt, as if we had been on holiday!

The date of 8 May was VE Day, the day on which Germany surrendered to the Allied forces. Since being released on 29 April, nine days previously, German forces had surrendered in Italy, Hitler had committed suicide, the Russians had conquered Berlin, the Americans and the Russians had met, officially, on the River Elbe at Torgau (which was near Stalag IVB), and the Germans in Holland, Denmark and northern Germany had capitulated to the British Army.

At the end of the day on Moosburg airfield, American soldiers took us over to some houses on its perimeter (which they had requisitioned at short notice), so we could bed down for the night. I felt sorry for the owners of the properties, as they had been moved out hastily and had had to leave everything as it was. For my part, I just slept on the floor, and at any rate there were too many of us to use the beds. Early the next morning we had to return to the airfield, but I'm sorry to say that this was not before some of our party had rifled the drawers and cupboards in the requisitioned house for souvenirs. I felt disgusted by this despoilment of someone's private home, by apparently otherwise disciplined men, who were shortly to be reunited with their own families and return to their own homes.

We had to wait a short time on the airfield for the Dakotas to arrive, so I had my last meal (breakfast) of Red Cross food, which I had saved for such an occasion. It was from an American parcel: a box of cornflakes and milk powder, which I managed to mix with water and eat in a comparatively civilised manner.

Not long afterwards, I was in the air on my way to Brussels, and what a feeling of elation I had! I don't recall much of the flight, but I remember noticing some of the German Autobahns with their bridges destroyed. When we arrived in Brussels, the city was enjoying its second VE Day (VE+1) celebrations (9 May), but all I wanted to do was to clean up and get a change of clothing. We were taken to a reception centre, where we registered and then had a shower. A bit like arriving at Stalag IVB, except we were all issued with new uniforms (and not our existing ones, deloused with gas!). After that we had a meal, with a band playing light music. One of the pieces performed was appropriately 'J'attendrai', and then we were allowed to go into the town. As we were returning to England the next day, and recent events had been quite exhausting for me, I decided to sleep in a proper bed for the first time in fifteen months, and save my celebrations for home.

The next day we left in small parties, with only room for a few passengers in each RAF Lancaster, and flew to RAF Odiham in Hampshire. We arrived to a heroes' welcome, with squadron leaders and wing commanders shaking our hands and offering to carry our kit to a hangar. This had been transformed into a large cafe, set out with tables and chairs, with the station WAAFs kept busy serving us tea and cakes, while an RAF band welcomed us with music.

After our refreshments we were each given a ten shilling note for our journey to RAF Cosford, in Shropshire. A party of us climbed into the back of an RAF open truck, which was to take us along the A30 to Paddington station in London. After some distance in open country we spied a large pub to the right of the road. We thumped on the side of the driver's cab for him to stop, and directed him to the building for a drink. It would be our first visit to a pub since we were shot down. But when we got to the entrance, there was a devastating notice, 'NO BEER'. Of course, we had arrived home after two days of victory celebrations, and the locals had drunk the place dry! Not to be outdone, we charged into the pub and, after explaining to the publican our plight, he pulled up some pints of ullage. They were floating with hops, but we didn't care, it was fine!

We followed this bout of 'drinking' with the invasion of a roadside cafe opposite the pub. We burst in, waving our ten shilling notes, asking for cups of tea. When they realised who we were, just back from Germany, they laid on a bit of a party for us! Naturally, we didn't break into our ten shilling notes, and it was great to be with British people, and back in our homeland again.

On our arrival in London, we stopped at the Endsleigh Hotel in Paddington for a meal. I took this opportunity to telephone my father from a pubic call box, using a free phone number. His first words to me were 'Are you all right?' My father had a colleague at work, whose son was an Army officer in Oflag VIIB (my second camp). He had been wounded in the shoot-up by the American Mustangs, and was left behind in the camp, liberated, and then repatriated by the Americans to a British hospital a few days later. And, of course, this incident of 'friendly fire' had been followed by a row about it in the House of Commons. I assured my father that I was OK and that I should be home in a few days' time.

We caught a train from Paddington to Cosford, shortly after our meal at the hotel. At Cosford, we were debriefed by intelligence officers, who had been instructed to record any possible atrocities that we might have experienced or witnessed in Germany. Some weeks beforehand, the Allied forces had overrun the German extermination camps where Jews had been interned (the Holocaust death camps). These had been filmed and shown in cinemas across Britain. The whole population had been repulsed by what they saw. As POWs we had not suffered such inhumane treatment. Germany had followed the Geneva Convention to what I would describe as a minimum extent. In Stalag IVB, there was excessive overcrowding and we lived in lice-ridden conditions, with no proper sewerage or waste-water systems. The food was not sufficient, and was of poor quality. Without the International Red Cross supplying food, and monitoring camps, life in prison camps would have been much worse, and many more of us would have died of illness and malnutrition.

Following our debriefing, we all had chest X-rays and full aircrew medicals. I was not able to 'blow up and hold' – I think, for one minute – a column of mercury, a critical test for aircrew. We were reissued with battledress and basic clothing and other kit. (I did not have an officer's kit, my commission having been promulgated while I was a POW, and I would have to get it from a military tailor while on leave.) After this we were issued with railway warrants and leave passes and we were free to go home! Not wanting to wait for transport to the railway station, a number of us hailed a passing lorry. It was an empty coal lorry. No matter, we couldn't wait, so we climbed aboard, kitbags and all.

I arrived back at Paddington in the late evening, too late to get a train home. Paddington was not far from Park Lane, and living in a deluxe flat in Fountain House in Park Lane was Mr Heron, the Boys' Brigade captain of a company I had belonged to before the war. He, his wife and daughter had been good friends of mine before the war, and between them had sent me twenty-six letters while I was in Stalag IVB. Mr Heron was the chief engineer of the Dorchester Hotel in Park Lane, and was living near the hotel because his house in Goodmayes (less than half a mile from where I had lived with my family) had been completely destroyed by a bomb in 1940. Mr and Mrs Heron were surprised indeed when I knocked on their door that evening. We talked almost the whole night through. They were the first personal friends I had spoken to for a long time.

The following morning I was on the last leg home. We had no telephone at home, and no neighbours who had one – not many people had the luxury of a phone in those days – so I could not tell my family I would be home soon.

I caught a train to Ilford station, and from there, a taxi home. It was nearly lunchtime, and my sisters and my father were at work. My mother must have had a premonition that it was I who was knocking on the door. She was already crying tears of joy – and was still holding the cabbage she had been preparing – when she opened the door.

Part Three
Aftermath

(*Previous page image*)
Reg and Barbara's wedding –
20 March 1954.

Chapter 10

Civvy Street and 'Normality'

Reg's account of his war experiences ended with his arrival back at his home in Goodmayes, Ilford, Essex. In June 1945, Reg, Johnny Bushell and George Griffiths attended the wedding of Laurie Underwood – reuniting the four surviving crew members – after which time they went their separate ways. Reg then slowly went back to life on Civvy Street. After being demobbed, he returned to work for Unilever Ltd in Blackfriars, London, in the same building he had been trying to reach on 30 December 1940 during the London Blitz, when he had vowed to join the RAF.

In September 1950, four and a half years after returning from internment in Germany, he met my mother, Barbara Spencer, on holiday on the Isle of Wight. However, he had to return from this holiday prematurely as his father had died unexpectedly. But before he left, he asked one of his friends to obtain Barbara's contact details, as he had taken a fancy to her! My mother once confessed that she had only accepted Reg's invitation for a date because she felt sorry that he had just lost his father. It wasn't exactly love at first sight from her point of view, although it obviously was for Reg! In any case, Reg's persistence paid off, and he and Barbara were married in St Mary's Church, Finchley, London, on 20 March 1954. Reg was thirty-one years old by this time, but Barbara was only twenty-four. After their wedding, my parents initially lived with my uncle and aunt in Newbury Park, Ilford, but then moved to their own newly built house in Chigwell, Essex, on 30 December 1954. This was fourteen years to the day since Reg had decided to volunteer for service in the RAF. By then, Barbara was heavily pregnant with her firstborn. Reg and Barbara lived in the same house in Chigwell for almost sixty years, finally relocating to the Dorset coast in 2014.

My brother, Robert, was born at Ilford maternity hospital on 15 March 1955, just before my parents' first wedding anniversary. I (Janet) followed on 17 January 1958, although I was born at home, in Chigwell. Our sister, Helen, was also born at home, on 21 May 1962.

So now Reg was a family man, with a good career. He had started out as an office junior after leaving school in 1939. He then had to start again 'at the bottom' after returning from military service in 1946, having been away in the RAF for some five years. By the time I was born, he had become an office systems specialist, and he eventually became an international management consultant. He remained with Unilever for the whole of his working life, finally retiring at the age of sixty-one in 1984.

Busy with his young family and a demanding job, which often involved travelling abroad, both within and beyond Europe, Reg had little time or inclination to reminisce about his war experiences. I can remember times when Robert and I were very small, possibly even before our sister Helen was born, climbing into our parents' enormous, squashy bed (or so it seemed to us). This was a rare treat, which was occasionally allowed on a Saturday or Sunday morning, when life was more relaxed. Once settled in this warm and welcoming haven, we would demand that our father should answer our favourite question: 'What did you do in the war, daddy?' Sometimes, he would tell us little titbits, like how he had saved his own life with a parachute, but for a long time we had absolutely no idea what he had been through. It was all a big adventure story in which our daddy was the hero. In fact, we probably still don't appreciate the full horror of what he experienced. Daddy's war tales were, to us, just a variation on the theme of 'tell us a story'. Our other favourite was *Jack and the Beanstalk*, which we loved because our father would really get into character when he did the voice of the giant! He *loved* growling, 'Fi, fie, foe, fum, I smell the blood of an Englishman! Be he alive or be he dead, I'll grind his bones to make my bread!' Perhaps these apparently trivial words had a deeper meaning for him. ...

I also remember, again as a small child, occasionally waking up to hear daddy shouting out in his sleep. I recall being afraid, and going to knock on the door of my parents' room, to enquire what was going on. My mother always said, 'It's all right now. Daddy has just had a bad dream. Go back to sleep now.' And I did. I never questioned it the next day. I just assumed that nightmares were something which all 'daddies' had to put up with.

In those days there was no counselling, or recognition of what one would now call 'post-traumatic stress syndrome'. There was no psychological help for Reg, who had probably witnessed things that were too awful to be recorded in his memoirs. In reality, he had been tormented for years by the knowledge that, although he had survived being shot down on 20 January 1944, four of his crewmembers had not escaped from the inferno. This included the wireless operator, Eric Church, who had helped Reg to kick out the jammed escape hatch, through which he had then successfully baled out just before the plane exploded. Two of his crewmembers had no known graves, as their remains, if found, had never been identified. Instead, they were remembered on the Runnymede Memorial, listed only as 'missing in action'. So their families, like very many others, had never been able to come to terms with their bereavement, and in some bizarre way Reg felt a sense of responsibility for this. It is a well-known syndrome. They call it survivors' guilt.

By the early 1970s I was studying modern languages, including German, and modern history. By the end of that decade I was studying languages at university. I vividly remember returning from a trip to Germany in July 1979, during which I had travelled alone by train from Frankfurt am Main to Berlin – when the Cold War was still a startling reality, and the Berlin Wall was a stark reminder of the legacy of the carving up of Germany by the Allied forces in 1945. I had crossed into East Berlin and had seen the extent of Soviet domination with my own, hitherto politically innocent, eyes. I was dying to talk about it. And there was Reg, who had fought in the Battle of Berlin, and who had incredible stories to tell, and he just couldn't share them with me! I thought he never would. But I was wrong.

There was a great resurgence of interest in the Second World War at the turn of the twentieth century. In June 1994, and again in June 2004, on the fiftieth and sixtieth anniversaries of D-Day and of the subsequent liberation of Europe, there was a huge amount of media coverage of the war and its aftermath. This included analysis of the Cold War and of the eventual dissolution of the grip of communism in eastern Europe, including the much fêted reunification of Germany, following the fall

of the Berlin Wall on 9 November 1989. The official day of German reunification was actually nearly a year later, on 3 October 1990. Perhaps
inspired and encouraged by these events, and having developed a growing
sense of time passing and the compelling need to share his fascinating
story with others, Reg began to talk and write about his experiences.

The reunification of Germany had enabled former East Germans to
explore for the first time the real history of their part of Germany in the
twentieth century, since the official view of history in the German
Democratic Republic (GDR) had naturally been coloured by communist
beliefs. Communism had been presented by the occupying Soviet powers
as the ideology that had saved East Germany from Nazism and there-
after from the evils of the capitalism that was seen to be blighting
the West.

In the wake of the reunification and the new-found freedom afforded
to former East Germans to explore their recent history, an association
was created to reunite former prisoners of Stalag IVB at Mühlberg am
Elbe, where Reg had been imprisoned from January 1944 until January
1945. So, in September 2001, Reg was at last able to go back to the site where
he and more than 46,000 others of many nationalities had suffered
imprisonment, and where, ironically, dissident East Germans had been
incarcerated by the Russians after the war. These dissident East German
prisoners had been interned in terrible conditions after the Soviet
takeover of eastern Germany, as by then the camp was even more
dilapidated than it had been at the end of the war. So East Germans had
faced terrible suffering there too. This meant that the reunion in 2001 was
not about 'us and them'. It was about 'us' and 'us'; fellow sufferers, albeit
under two very different and perhaps equally evil regimes. (It is ironic
that this event occurred just days before the horrific terrorist attack in
New York on 9/11; an attack that served to remind us that the world is
still a troubled place, where terrorism is alive and well. What have we
learned? We may have peace in Europe, but in other parts of the world,
life is far from tranquil.)

I believe that Reg's visit to Mühlberg in 2001, together with the heart
attack he suffered in May 2002, gave him the impetus to finally sit down
and write coherently about his experiences, using the notes he had
originally made in April 1945 as the war drew to a close. To this, he had

added other information that he had gleaned during the course of his modern-day research. The following chapters are an edited version of Reg's post-war recollections and observations.

Chapter 11

Reg Remembers

I became a member of the Caterpillar Club soon after the end of the Second World War. For this to happen, I needed to register with them the fact that I had saved my life, having baled out of an aircraft that was on fire and out of control. In free fall, I had manually pulled the ripcord of my Irving parachute, which released its canopy and supporting shroud lines.

Barbara and I had been invited to the Biggin Hill air show in 2003. The invitation was extended to a number of Caterpillar Club members who resided in the London area, and was hosted in a VIP marquee at the air show.

In 1922, Irving, the designer of the modern parachute, had decided to form a club of those who had saved their lives by means of such a parachute. Irving named it the Caterpillar Club and by 1945 there were 34,000 members. (The caterpillar is symbolic of the silk worm, which descends gently to the earth from great heights by spinning a silky thread from which to hang. Silk was also the fabric that parachutes were originally made from.) The Irving Parachute Company gives every member a certificate, a gold tie pin and a lapel pin, shaped like a caterpillar. The caterpillar has red eyes if the aircraft from which the member had jumped was on fire. The recipient's name and rank are engraved on the reverse of the tie pin.

In August 1994, Barbara and I attended the annual memorial service at the Runnymede War Memorial, arranged by the Aircrew Association. This was particularly important to me as we were able to view the names of two of the four members of my crew: flight engineer John Bremner and mid-upper gunner Charles Dupueis, who were both killed and who had no known graves at that time. Their names had been recorded within the cloisters of the memorial, and 1994 was the fiftieth anniversary year of their deaths. The memorial lists some 22,000 names of RAF personnel without known graves, who were killed in the Second World War.

After we had all been demobbed in 1946, the ensuing years were spent developing our careers and getting on with our lives. I had returned to Unilever in 1946 and eventually became a management consultant. George Griffiths continued flying as a pilot in a civilian air transport company and then as a senior captain with British Airways. Laurie studied accountancy and eventually, as a sales manager of Philips, at first sold mechanised, and later computerised, accountancy equipment. Johnny Bushell developed tuberculosis shortly after the war, contracted as a result of poor conditions in Stalag IVB. Following the partial removal of one of his lungs, he was awarded a full war disability pension. However, he was still able to work and became a housing officer for Bedford Council. Johnny remained a bachelor, but George, Laurie and I married and raised families, which gave us little time to muse about our wartime experiences.

We exchanged Christmas cards, and I occasionally visited Laurie and John in the course of my business travels around the UK. However, we hadn't met up as a group since shortly after the war. I had lost contact with George Griffiths until, sometime in the 1970s, I managed to locate his wife's parents in Craven Arms, Shropshire, and they gave me his address. He was still serving with British Airways when, one year, I phoned him at precisely 8 o'clock GMT on 20 January (the anniversary of the exact time when we were shot down). This became an annual event, and subsequently we contacted each other every year by this means, commemorating our lucky survival.

I retired in 1984 and George, who lived in Ruislip, retired some time later. Barbara and I managed to visit him on occasions when we stayed over at Northolt to see Barbara's mother – this was in the early 1990s. During his retirement, George had spent time researching at the RAF Museum at Hendon, and had obtained photographs and some information about the remaining four members of our crew. They had all been killed. Two were buried in the 1939–45 Berlin War Cemetery, and two were remembered on the Runnymede Memorial, as they had no known graves. Also, with the help of a German archivist, George had obtained details of how and where we were brought down. We were not shot down by flak, or hit by a bomb falling through our wing from one of the Allied aircraft above, as we first thought, but by an ace night-fighter pilot. The archivist had also traced the crash point of our plane in Berlin. In support of this information, he had sent George a photograph and some biographical details about the night-fighter pilot who had shot us down. In addition, there was a map of the exact point where some of the debris of the Halifax had fallen. (George had landed in waste ground, among the wreckage, and was able to recall the name of an underground railway station that he and his captors had walked past shortly after he was apprehended.)

In retirement, I had finally had time to read several books about Bomber Command and the Berlin raids. My reading, together with the information George had shared with me, caused me to start thinking again about what I had experienced fifty years beforehand. The subject had always been there in my subconscious mind, but everything was now coming to the surface again.

The four surviving members of my crew arranged to meet at a Peterborough hotel on our fiftieth anniversary in 1994. The purpose of the reunion was to celebrate the extra fifty years of life we had enjoyed because of an arbitrary quirk of fate. Why had we survived? Why not the others? Present at the celebration were myself, Reg (navigator), George Griffiths, also known as GAG or 'Griff' (pilot), John Bushell, or Johnny to his friends (rear gunner) and Laurie Underwood (bomb aimer). The location in Peterborough was chosen because it was a central location and was therefore reasonably accessible to the four survivors of 'Old Flo'. We dined and raised our glasses 'to absent friends' at the exact hour (8.00 p.m. GMT, 20 January) when we had been shot down. This was our first meeting as a group since June 1945!

As previously mentioned, by this time George Griffiths had begun some research at the RAF Museum in Hendon, and with their help had obtained a map from the German authorities, showing the approximate location of the crash site of our plane. (This map proved to be a crucial element in events that were to unfold much later). George had also ascertained the name of the ace fighter pilot who had shot down our Halifax bomber that fateful night. He was Hauptmann Leopold Fellerer or 'Poldi', and his enormous success in shooting down enemy aircraft had led to his being awarded the Knight's Cross (das Ritterkreuz) in February 1944. This followed his amazing feat of bringing down five enemy bombers, including our plane, in one night; an event much fêted by the Luftwaffe, and the subject of a propaganda newsreel that can now be viewed on You Tube: *https://www.youtube.com/watch?v=FCzTzenwliI*

A cousin of Laurie Underwood, on hearing about our reunion, had contacted the BBC, and they arranged for a TV team and a radio car to attend our meeting in the afternoon prior to our dinner. We were asked to bring with us any memorabilia we had, which meant that we were all able to fill in a number of gaps in our knowledge.

Johnny and I learned how George, when the plane was on fire over Berlin, had been held in his seat by G-force, with his head thrust forward and the throttle levers behind his ears, when the plane went into a spiral dive. He described his vivid recollection of seeing the altimeter 'unwind' from 17,000 feet through to 7,000 feet before he blacked out. He regained consciousness and found himself in the open air and in free fall, after the plane's fuel tanks had exploded and he had been blown out of the aircraft. The splinters of Plexiglas that lacerated his face suggested that he had been propelled by the explosion through a hatch in the cupola above his head. (This was a feature of Halifax bombers, which Lancaster bombers did not have. Although Lancaster bombers were always considered to be superior to Halifaxes, because they could fly higher and carry heavier bombloads, it is also the case that, once hit, one was more likely to get out of a Halifax alive. The existence of the hatch above George's head almost certainly saved his life.) By the time he pulled his ripcord, George had been only a few hundred feet from the ground. His parachute opened, but was still 'on the swing' when he hit terra firma, with the debris of the aircraft around him. Although in shock, he landed virtually unscathed.

Laurie told Johnny and me how, immediately after arriving at Stalag Luft III in Poland in February 1944, he was recruited as an extra look-out while they completed the escape tunnel 'Harry' for the Great Escape.

Laurie, being a latecomer, was not included in the escape. In fact, he was lucky, as fifty of the seventy-six who did abscond, and who were then recaptured, were murdered on the direct orders of Hitler. Laurie and George, like me, had had to march away from their prison camp as the 'front line' drew closer at the end of January 1945. In their case, it was from Russian troops, who were approaching from the Eastern Front. They marched in freezing conditions and were then entrained on 2 February to Marlag-Milag camp, where they stayed until 10 April. They then marched again for two weeks across northern Germany. They were liberated a week later, on 2 May 1945, just south of Lübeck, on the Baltic, by the British Army.

Thus, by the end of our celebrations at Peterborough, we had learned much more about each other's experiences. The BBC made a three-minute video about the reunion, which was broadcast via Yorkshire and Look East television companies on the eight o'clock news that night. George and I were interviewed in a BBC radio van, and a three-minute recording of the interview went out from Cambridge as well. The interview proved to be so popular that it was broadcast three times.

Following the reunion, I finally felt able to begin to record some of my experiences in Bomber Command, and to assemble various documents, together with letters I had received after being shot down, and other arte-facts. The catharsis had finally begun.

In June 1995, it being Laurie's golden wedding anniversary, we all met again, this time in Laurie's home town of Wetherby in Yorkshire. After the celebrations, we took the opportunity of visiting the Yorkshire Air Museum at Elvington, which was a satellite airfield to RAF Pocklington during the war. At that time, they were in the process of rebuilding a Halifax Mark III bomber to represent the most famous wartime Halifax, 'Friday 13th', which clocked up 128 bombing missions. The plane had been displayed on Horse Guards Parade in London after the war, but then it was broken up. In contrast, one Lancaster bomber has a place of honour in the RAF Battle of Britain Memorial Flight, and another is displayed in the RAF Museum at Hendon for all time.

There were over 6,000 Halifax aircraft built during the war. They were used for over 80,000 bombing and mine-laying missions in Europe in

Bomber Command, and supported the other armed forces on D-Day and in the ensuing liberation of Europe. They operated in the Middle East, and also in Coastal Command, attacking U-boats in the North Sea and in the North Atlantic. In addition, they towed airborne troops in gliders to Normandy on D-Day and later to Arnhem in the Netherlands and, in the final stages of the war, to the crossing of the Rhine.

In my opinion, it beggars belief that any Government would scrap every Halifax built, taking into account their contribution to the success of the Second World War and their place in history, but that is what happened. It was not until 1983 that there was enough historical interest to consider restoring a Halifax bomber in the UK. As Yorkshire had been the 'birth-place' and wartime home of the aircraft, it was natural that the Yorkshire Air Museum would take on the task. In 1984, they found the fuselage of a Halifax that had crashed in the Hebrides in 1945. It had been bought by a farmer and used as a hen house! This fuselage was acquired by the museum and moved to Yorkshire. Parts were collected from almost all corners of the world. Pieces from at least three Halifax aircraft were used: the wings came from a post-war Hastings and the engines were donated by the French Air Force (who flew Halifax bombers from Elvington in 1943). The nose section had to be rebuilt from scratch with the help of British Aerospace, aided by volunteer engineers. When we visited the museum in 1995, the aircraft was still only partially assembled. It was some years later before it was completed and it is now on display, as 'Friday 13th', in its own hangar. As far as I know, contributions to its construction, both in terms of effort and cost, were all voluntary; no Government money was ever offered to help with this venture.

Mainly for the benefit of Laurie and George, we also made the most of our visit to Yorkshire to visit another local museum. The site of this museum was originally a British POW camp for German prisoners of war and it was subsequently converted into a museum to commemorate the Second World War. One of its exhibits was a replica of the escape tunnel code-named 'Harry', which was used at Stalag Luft III for the escape of seventy-six RAF prisoners (fifty of whom were murdered when recaptured). The tunnel was of particular interest, as it displayed the pump system for providing ventilation and the novel trolley mechanism for moving the escapees along its whole length, to the end of the tunnel.

On 23 December 1995, the *Daily Mail* featured a double-page spread showing life in Stalag IVB and, in particular, what had happened there at Christmas in 1944, when American prisoners of war had arrived. Having been taken prisoner at the Battle of the Bulge, they were in a very sorry state, physically and mentally. The article had been supplied by Tom Nelson (and it included a large photograph of him). I did not know Tom Nelson in Stalag IVB, as he had been in another barracks block while I was there. But I did meet him in Oflag VIIB when we were both moved to this camp in February 1945. We shared the same room with two Australian Army chaps, until we marched out on 15 April 1945. Apart from a chance meeting, and saying a fleeting hello in London in 1946, I had not seen him since our liberation at the end of April 1945.

I got in touch with the *Daily Mail*, and they agreed to forward my letter to him, but they would not give me his address. My letter included photocopies of my drawings of Oflag VIIB, which were from my wartime logbook. Of particular interest was a drawing of 'our room', which he and I had signed, along with our two Australian colleagues.

A week or so later I received a phone call (which was at least two hours long) from an amazed Tom Nelson. He said his memory of Oflag VIIB was a bit hazy, but the signature on the drawing was definitely his own, and we agreed to meet at the RAF Club in Piccadilly, to reminisce and to renew our friendship.

After Tom was demobbed, he worked for several American airlines in flight operations, and married Pat, an American. He spent time in America and Germany and returned to the UK to run a travel agency. It was then that he joined the Stalag IVB ex-POW Group and attended their annual reunions in Edinburgh. As a result, he had collected photographs, drawings, poems and various records about IVB. He brought these along to the RAF Club, and I was able to copy them.

The most important information I learned from him was what had happened to the Mühlberg Stalag IVB camp site in 1945, after this area of Germany became part of the Russian Zone. At first, Stalag IVB ex-Kriegies, visiting the site after the war, were told by the Russians or East Germans that it had been occupied by German refugees with nowhere to live. Allegedly, with barracks, electricity and water available, they had made it 'their home'. These stories turned out to be completely untrue.

The reality was that the camp had become Special Internment Camp No. 1 (with even more barbed wire than Stalag IVB around it). In this camp, Germans who were considered to be a danger to the stability of the Soviet state were interned without any evidence or trial. They were not allowed visitors, parcels, or help of any sort, and were not able to communicate with anybody outside the camp. In a short time it became a filthy, disease-ridden place. This camp remained open until November 1948, during which time about 22,000 victims of communist oppression passed through it. Some 6,700 of them died of starvation or disease in this period and were buried in mass graves, just north-east of what had previously been the RAF compound when I was there. Many others were moved to camps in the Soviet Union, and were never heard of again. All this information was withheld from the general population, and those who did know the truth were threatened with severe punishment if they disclosed it.

Following the decommissioning of the camp in 1948, the Russians removed all the wooden barracks for use as workers' huts elsewhere. Other structures were sold to local farmers. In the end, nothing was left except the concrete foundations of the washhouses, the barracks, the forty-holer latrines and the static water 'reservoirs'. The Russians had tried to disguise the site of the former camp by planting birch trees all over it. Consequently, the site soon became overgrown with vegetation.

After the Russians left, and when East and West Germany had been re-unified, the lies and cloak of secrecy were exposed. Many of the relatives of those who died in the camp subsequently visited the site. They have put crosses in the area of the mass graves and the place has become a shrine, with its own memorial.

I was grateful to Tom for sharing this information with me. We met several times over the course of the next few years at the RAF Club. Later on, Tom began to suffer from double vision and could no longer travel on his own. However, he did put me in contact with the Stalag IVB ex-POW Group, which by now was much depleted. With fewer remaining members, they had moved their meeting point south, to Peterborough.

In 2000, the son of a member of Stalag IVB ex-POW Group, Tony Drewitt, offered to organise a visit to Mühlberg and the Stalag IVB site, which was enthusiastically taken up by the members of the Group. This included Tom Nelson, Johnny Bushell and myself.

In 1944 Tony Drewitt's father, Harry Drewitt, had lost his best friend in IVB, when the latter had been shot dead by a guard as he leaned over the trip wire to pick some wild strawberries. In recent years Tony and his family had been to Germany, and had visited Mühlberg's Stalag IVB site and the Berlin 1939–45 War Cemetery. Harry Drewitt's friend, and all those British and Commonwealth POWs who died in Stalag IVB are now buried there, having been transferred from the neighbouring Neuburxdorf cemetery.

During their visits to the Stalag IVB site, the Drewitt family met Mayor Brendel and others who, since 1990 and the reunification of Germany, have openly publicised the atrocities perpetrated in Mühlberg Special Internment Camp No. 1 (previously Stalag IVB). For this purpose, they formed the Mühlberg Initiative Group, to make the Mühlberg camp into a permanent memorial. They have cleaned up the main road through it, marking out the various areas of the camp, and showing where the mass graves and the memorial of the Special Camp No. 1 are situated. Where possible, they have revealed the foundations of the cookhouses, barracks' washhouses and latrines, which is all that is now left of the original camp.

Mayor Brendel and the Mühlberg Initiative Group welcomed the idea that a party of British ex-POWs and families might wish to visit the site, and said that Mühlberg would like to host the visit. Every year ex-Kriegies from Poland, France and other countries visit the Neuburxdorf cemetery. About 4,000 POWs who died in IVB were buried here originally. It now has a war memorial to represent all the nations that had citizens imprisoned there. Visits to the camp are now combined with the service for the German civilian post-war victims who died in the Special Internment Camp No. 1.

For the British visit in 2001, Tony Drewitt agreed with Mayor Brendel that she would arrange the hotel accommodation in Mühlberg, and host an evening dinner with the Initiative Group. The date coincided with the remembrance services at Neuburxdorf cemetery and Mühlberg camp site. Coaches were provided for all the planned visits.

Over ninety ex-POWs, family and friends, including Tom Nelson, Johnny Bushell, Barbara and myself, took part in the visit, which commenced on 6 September 2001. We flew from London Stansted into Berlin's most modern airport, Schönefeld, which is only a short distance from where our Halifax crashed in 1944.

We were taken in two coaches to Treff Park Hotel, about 6 miles south-east of the Brandenburg Gate. After dinner there was a coach tour of central Berlin. Although the tour was impromptu, with a helpful but inexpert guide, it was sufficient to give us a glimpse of the contrasts between East and West. We had a passing view of the main shopping centres, which showed that the East looked relatively deprived, with poor buildings, displays and lighting, when compared with the West. We viewed the famous graffiti on the remains of the Berlin Wall and, at my request, the new Kaiser Wilhelm Memorial Church alongside the ruins of the old one. The original church was destroyed on 22 November 1943, during the second Berlin raid in which I took part. It is a similar memorial to that of Coventry Cathedral, which was destroyed in 1940.

The following morning we were taken to the 1939–45 British War Cemetery, in which are buried nearly 2,900 RAF aircrew who were killed during the Battle of Berlin and in other raids on eastern Germany. (Only 800 of the 4,000 who were shot down in the Battle of Berlin survived this operation – John and I are two of these). Many whole crews are buried there together, in lines of seven graves, which lead up to the Stone of Remembrance and on as far as the central cross.

The cemetery is situated in an area of woodland that is part of the Grünewald Forest in the district of Charlottenburg. It is beautifully maintained, as are all British war graves. Barbara and I, together with Johnny Bushell, spent some time locating and placing poppies on the graves of two of our crewmembers who are buried here: F/S K.F. Stanbridge (co-pilot), and P/O E. Church (wireless operator). Our search was not a straightforward one, as their graves were not side by side, but at opposite ends of the cemetery. We found Ken Stanbridge's grave first, and I remembered that Ken had passed George Griffith's parachute to him, not long before the aircraft went into a spiral dive. George lived and Ken didn't. Visiting Eric Church's grave also had a particular significance for me, as he had helped Laurie Underwood and me to kick out the jammed escape hatch, and he should have followed us out. But the plane must have gone into the spiral dive immediately after we had baled out, and he had no chance to follow us; just a few seconds, separating life and death. ... George, Laurie, John and I were incredibly lucky to survive.

Following these personal visits to the graves of former colleagues, Reverend Michael Whelton (a friend of Tony Drewitt who was acting as the 'padre' for the party) held a short but emotional service. Then a wreath was placed on the Stone of Remembrance, before we continued our itinerary to the centre of Berlin. I was deeply grateful that Johnny and I had finally been able to make this trip to the cemetery after so many years, as it closed a chapter in my mind.

In Berlin, we first visited the Brandenburg Gate. This also had some significance for me, for it was at 18,000 feet above here that we were attacked by a night fighter and shot down in 1944. Our target had been Hitler's Chancery, which was just south of the Gate. Our second visit was to the Reichstag, a short distance away. The Reichstag was not destroyed during the Second World War. After the reunification of East and West Germany in October 1990, when Berlin became the capital of the newly reunified Germany, it was once again used to house the German Parliament. It was renovated by the British architect, Sir Norman Foster, who had been specially chosen to do the work. His idea was to enlarge the Plenary Hall and add a new modern glass cupola, from which the public could view Parliament in action – its main feature. The task was completed in 1999. Although the cupola could be seen from outside the building, we didn't have time to go inside to view it on that occasion, before we continued our journey south to Mühlberg.

We travelled about 75 miles to Mühlberg, through mostly open countryside, passing several buildings or barracks that were once occupied by the Russians, and were now in a dilapidated state. Mühlberg is a small town on the River Elbe, noted for its numerous Renaissance buildings, which luckily escaped damage when the Russians advanced through it on their way to Berlin in April 1945. Today, naturally, the town is also remembered for its close proximity to the former prison camp.

On arrival we were met by Mayor Brendel and a number of helpers, who took us to our small hotels or private accommodation, which was dotted around the town. In the evening, we were invited to a reception in the town hall, organised by Mayor Brendel and the Mühlberg Initiative Group.

In the address, it was explained that Initiative Groups were formed all over Germany after the reunification in 1990, by survivors of the Special Internment Camps, in order to remember and make known the atrocities perpetrated by the Russians during their occupation. To this end, the Initiative Groups have preserved sites like Mühlberg, Buchenwald and Sachsenhausen, and have set up small museums, containing documents and photographs, so that younger generations will be properly informed about these dark days of their history. To these memories of Soviet oppression, they have added details of the wartime atrocities of the Nazi era. In Mühlberg they have also included information about Stalag IVB, as it is known that hundreds of thousands of POWs from all over the world, when passing through the camp from 1939 to 1945, suffered from cold, damp, overcrowding, poor and inadequate food and lack of hygiene. There were many deaths, many more than those recorded in the Neuburxdorf cemetery, including thousands of Russian POWs who died of typhus in the early years of the war and were buried elsewhere.

The following day, we visited the small Mühlberg museum, which had records, drawings and artefacts donated by ex-POWs from IVB. This was followed by a lunch of soup, goulash and hunks of bread and coffee, which was warming and very welcome, and was provided by the town fire service.

In the afternoon we were taken in coaches to Neuburxdorf, and we viewed the railway sidings where all the POWs, including myself, had disembarked from their cattle trucks for their march to the sinister Stalag IVB in the middle of the flat fields of Saxony. I recall that the ground was covered with slushy snow when I arrived there, and that the camp looked as if it were in Siberia, such was the bleakness of its aspect.

After this visit we proceeded to the Neuburxdorf cemetery to attend the annual memorial service for all the POWs of many nationalities who died in IVB and who were buried here. During this service, our ex-POW Stalag IVB Group dedicated a plaque, which was laid in the cemetery as a memorial to the sixty RAF POWs who were buried there and who were subsequently removed to the Berlin site. The plaque was donated by the Canadian Air Force.

To complete the day's visits we travelled the short distance to the Stalag

IVB site. We drove through what was originally the east gate. The Lagerstrasse or main road was still there, but was now flanked by birch trees and undergrowth that covered the whole site. As described earlier, the Mühlberg Initiative Group and associates had cleared some parts of the camp to reveal the concrete foundations of washhouses and latrines. They had marked out the areas of the various compounds and the two cookhouses. As my barracks was close to the French cookhouse, Barbara, John, Tom and I were able to locate the area of the barracks, but due to the undergrowth we were unable to reach it. But we were able to get to the site of our forty-holer latrine, which still had (though somewhat crumbled) the concrete foundation and septic tank below. Its four open channels in the concrete base remained intact. Over each channel there had been a long wooden rectangular box, serving as a seat, with ten holes in it, so forty of us could be there at one sitting!

We were only a short distance away from the mass burial site of the victims of Special Camp No. 1, just a few yards to the north-east of us. There is now a large cross erected there as a memorial to the 6,700 German detainees who died of starvation and disease in the period between 1945 and 1948. Among the undergrowth, near the cross, there were many smaller crosses put there by relatives and friends over the course of the previous few years.

We joined the Mühlberg Initiative Group again, with relations and friends of several nationalities, for their annual service of remembrance at the memorial. Then we made a further inspection of the remnants of the camp, nearer the west gate entrance, before returning in our coaches to Mühlberg.

So we said goodbye to the site of Stalag IVB and Special Camp No. 1. It was now a sleeping forest of birch trees, encapsulating the memories and miseries of probably hundreds of thousands of prisoners from many nations, who passed through it during the war years and their aftermath. On our return to Mühlberg, we attended yet another memorial service in the church, just for ourselves this time, before we had our evening meal in the town hall. This was followed by Lew Parsons (our chairman) giving a slide presentation of photographs of Stalag IVB to local people, including some older children, who afterwards asked us questions about the camp and the Second World War.

In Zeithain, the Initiative Group had built a wooden hut to illustrate the type of barracks used to house POWs. We had to criticise it, as it did not illustrate the full horror of the conditions under which prisoners had to live. It had no rickety three-tier bunks; it was neither overcrowded nor dilapidated; it had no floor of bricks set in earth; and it did not indicate the unhygienic state of our surroundings! In Zeithain, they also had a small museum, which included photographs showing guards and others, mistreating and punishing prisoners.

After several more trips, we arrived back in Stansted on the evening of 10 September, after a very busy and successful tour. Only a few hours later, we were to learn of the atrocities perpetrated by terrorists in New York on '9/11'. These were to change the course of modern history once more. Tom Nelson and his American wife both knew New York well, and were very upset about what happened. Sadly, Tom, who had not been completely fit for some time, died suddenly later that year, in November 2001.

Stalag IVB reunions were held in Peterborough every year over the weekend nearest to 23 April, which was the day the camp was liberated by the Russians. Barbara and I attended these from 2002 to 2005. (Saturday 23 April 2005 was the fiftieth anniversary of the liberation day.) Each year's reunion ended with a rousing rendition of 'Land of Hope and Glory'. It had been sung in IVB, in place of the national anthem, which was disallowed. In September 2005, there was a further reunion, back in Mühlberg. This time, one of our grandsons, Christopher, accompanied us on the trip, about which more detail is given in Chapter 12.

After my eightieth birthday in 2003 I decided that, for the sake of my children and grandchildren, I should claim my medals. According to my assessment, I was entitled to four of these. (If Bomber Command had ever been awarded a campaign medal, it would have been five.) Air Chief Marshal Sir Arthur Harris once said that 'Every butcher, baker, and candlestick maker within 200 miles of the front got a campaign medal … but not the men of Bomber Command.' The post-war Government was embarrassed about the heavy loss of life in the bombing of Dresden, and the aircrews got the blame for it. This situation was compounded by Harris's unpopularity in the period immediately after the war, when he became a scapegoat. This was in the wake of the criticism regarding the morality, or otherwise, of area bombing. In the period before the general election, in the summer of 1945, even Winston Churchill, once a staunch ally of Arthur Harris, distanced himself from Bomber Command, to the point where they did not even get a mention in his victory speech. Churchill was not going to risk going against public feelings, which were, by now, running high in the wake of the 'unjustifiable' bombing of Dresden in February 1945. Churchill wanted votes, not vilification. As a result of his stance, a campaign medal was not granted to Bomber Command aircrew, despite their courage and dedication in carrying out high-risk bombing operations, night after night, right up until the end of the war. Bomber Command aircrews, mostly in their early twenties, carried out orders in a climate of total war, and suffered the highest casualties of all the British and Commonwealth forces during the whole of the Second World War. This fact is rarely publicised.

For my part, my entitlement to medals finally amounted to three, as the fourth medal, the Defence Medal, required three years' non-active service. After deducting eleven and a half months of training time abroad, I could only muster two years and nine months, even after adding my Home Guard duties before I joined the RAF. The rest of my war service (one year and three months) was as a POW, and this counted for nothing – as I was duly informed by an officious civil servant in the Medal Agency. In America, however, there was an additional medal, which was awarded specifically to those who had been POWs.

So I was only deemed to be entitled to the following medals:

- 1939–45 Star – for active service.
- Aircrew Europe Star – for aircrew active service (Europe 1939–D-Day 1944).
- War Medal – for general service.

Part Four
Achieving Closure

(*Previous page image*)
Reg Wilson solemnly stands
behind the sister of his fellow
Bomber Command airman,
John Bremner, at the burial
of John's remains. 16 October
2008.

Chapter 12

2005 – the Quest Begins

In September 2005, my father Reg was due to go back to Mühlberg for a second visit, together with Barbara, for a 'sixty years since the liberation' reunion at Stalag IVB. Finance had been received for this trip under the auspices of the 'Heroes Return' initiative, funded by the National Lottery. The fund enabled Second World War veterans, like Reg, to take part in commemorative visits to mark events that had led to the end of the war. He wanted me to accompany him and my mother as their 'carer', both because he knew that I had a passionate interest in his story, and because of my ability to communicate on his behalf in German, as I am a teacher of French and German. Then I got a new teaching job, and as this was due to start in early September, I couldn't go. Reg was bitterly disappointed and so was I! My son, Christopher, then aged seventeen, accompanied them instead. This was poignant for Reg, as Christopher was almost exactly of the age Reg had been when – experiencing the London Blitz – he had vowed to train as a pilot. During the excursion, which was a great success, Chris became really engaged in his grandfather's story. Meeting Reg's POW 'mucker' and former rear gunner, Johnny Bushell, and visiting the site of the camp for himself, had made his Grandpa's story suddenly come to life. Chris also became popular with all the veterans on the trip, as he kept informing them about the latest cricket scores, which he was obtaining by means of text updates on his mobile phone. This was, of course, the month of the famous Ashes series, when England finally got their own back against the Australians. The Aussies had held the Ashes since 1987, the year before Christopher's birth, so this was news indeed!

Not being able to participate in the trip really bothered me at the time. I felt guilty that I could not accompany my father on this important and historic visit, although it is fair to say that I would not have been as good a cricket commentator as my son! As a way to appease my conscience for my inability to accompany him on the trip, and to make Reg feel better about things, I promised to take him back to Berlin at the next possible opportunity, which was during the October half-term holiday.

Reg wanted to find out exactly where his plane had crashed. He had some knowledge, but it was incomplete. The information had been obtained by Reg's late pilot, George Griffiths, who had continued his career after the war, first by taking part in the historic Berlin Airlift, and later as a pilot in civil aviation. On his retirement, George, who lived in West London near the RAF Museum at Hendon, had done some research via the museum. The archivists had managed to obtain the name of the Messerschmitt fighter pilot who had shot down his plane, using contemporary German records. The German pilot was the Knight's Cross holder, Hauptmann Leopold Fellerer, or 'Poldi' to his friends. The archivists had also provided George with a map showing the approximate position of the crash site, although this was only a poor photocopy of the original. George had given Reg a copy of the map (by now a second- or third-generation photocopy) at their meeting in 1994, on the fiftieth anniversary of their incredible escape. George sadly died on 14 June 1998, after a short illness. He was seventy-five years old. (His own story is told in a book entitled *Spared Again*).

So it had fallen to Reg to continue the research, if he chose to do so. In 1994, after the fifty-year reunion, he had begun to jot down a few notes. Receiving the map and the details of the Messerschmitt pilot from George Griffiths had begun to awaken in him a deep-seated desire to fill in the gaps in his knowledge. His thirst for new information increased in 2001, when he visited the site of his former POW camp at Mühlberg. In May 2002, a few months before his eightieth birthday, and four years after the death of his pilot, Reg survived a heart attack, and this made him think hard about his own mortality. At this point, he began to bring together the information from his own diaries, and that which he had pieced together from his more recent meetings and reunions. George Griffiths could no longer pursue his quest for information, but Reg could. The warm reception that he and Barbara had received during their visit to his former POW camp in 2001 had also made him aware that the

Germans of the twenty-first century, far from being hostile to his enquiries, would be likely to help him in his research. He observed that the former East Germans, newly liberated from the shackles of communist censorship, were particularly keen to research their recent history and heritage.

Reg became increasingly proficient in using the Internet; a true 'Silver Surfer'! With the impending return trip to Mühlberg on the cards, he had announced his ambition to find the actual crash site of his wartime Halifax. I tried to discourage him and said: 'Dad, it's sixty-one years ago. Even if it is still there, they'll have built a factory or something on it by now. It's like looking for a needle in a haystack!' However, Reg was by now like a terrier reluctant to relinquish a bone. He just would not give up. I now believe that this was the moment of his second calling. It was another leap of faith, this time into metaphorical darkness, for in spite of the huge odds stacked against him and the very slim chance of being successful in his quest, he felt a deep-seated need to answer this call.

And that is how, one afternoon in July 2005, with his second visit to his former POW camp on the horizon, Reg enlisted my help in comparing his poorly photocopied map, showing the approximate site of the crash, with the satellite images on Google Earth. After some time, we concluded that if the cross on the map had been accurately placed, the plane had probably crashed in a wooded area. Furthermore, this area of woodland was still visible on the satellite image of the outskirts of Berlin. It seemed to be to Berlin what Epping Forest is to London. This was ironic, as my parents then lived on the fringe of Epping Forest. We began to speculate whether any German planes had ever crashed in Epping Forest on their way to bomb London. (In fact, I have since then found several references to such events on the Internet).

After some further research into historical associations in modern Berlin, Reg identified a small local museum in Köpenick, the district southeast of Berlin that encompassed what we believed to be the approximate crash site. He then contacted the museum's curator and archivist, the late Claus-Dieter Sprink, who put Reg in touch with a journalist named Ralf Drescher, about whom more later. Claus-Dieter had replied to Reg's email, and was keen to help him with his research. An engineer by training, Claus-Dieter had developed, initially as a hobby, a passionate interest in local history, which had been facilitated by the reunification of Germany. He also had a particularly personal reason for wanting to seek out the truth, having earlier been persecuted by the Stasi (East German Secret Police) and imprisoned as an enemy of the state. It is also possible that he had been tortured during his captivity, although he never spoke openly about this. There is interesting, if somewhat anecdotal, evidence that the communists tortured 'trouble makers' such as Claus-Dieter, and even some suggestion that they were deliberately exposed to high levels of radiation, as the incidence of deaths from cancer among former 'enemies of the state' is exceptionally high. Tragically, Claus-Dieter died of cancer on 4 October 2006, aged fifty-one, and so went to his grave – which I have since visited – unaware of the incredible long-term legacy of his efforts to help us with our research.

In the summer of 2005, thanks to Claus-Dieter, a campaign had been launched on our behalf in several Berlin newspapers. Ralf Drescher became incredibly important to us at this point, as a freelance investigative journalist and photographer. Ralf's first article in the newspaper *Berliner Woche* in 2005 attracted a large number of readers. Incredibly, over sixty people contacted the newspaper to share their experiences as witnesses of some of the most traumatic moments in Berlin's troubled history. On 26 October, we visited what we then thought was the crash site of Reg's plane, and spoke to potential eyewitness, Siegfried Gall. His information was useful and enlightening, but not conclusive. He had certainly seen the wreckage of a plane, but his knowledge was hazy. He told of the sighting by local residents in the woodland of men 'in underwear', who were believed to have escaped from a crashed plane. Reg decided that these were probably airmen from another crashed bomber, who had stripped off their parachutes and RAF uniforms in the hope that they would be able to hide their identity if they were only wearing their thermals when they were captured!

When we visited the site and met with Siegfried Gall, my son Christopher, then aged seventeen, had been taken aside by a journalist who had specifically wanted to hear his view of recent events. This was Chris's second excursion to Germany in a matter of weeks, as he had also accompanied his grandparents on their trip to Mühlberg and Berlin in early September. The journalist asked Chris how he felt about modern Germany and the Germans whom he had encountered during his trip. Chris replied, without any hesitation, that they had all behaved with the utmost respect and courtesy, and that they had been among the friendliest people whom he had met anywhere. He also added that there was never any hint of animosity or resentment by the Germans against their former enemies. This was not just a sound-bite. It came straight from the heart, and was promptly transcribed by the journalist and used in her article.

The eyewitness, Siegfried Gall, had suggested that Allied airmen who were shot down would want to disguise their identity from civilians, even if they intended to give themselves up to the military authorities. He was probably right about this, as it is known that many airmen who were caught by civilians before they had had a chance to attempt escape, or to surrender to officials, were murdered in cold blood. It depended very much on the type of person who found them. As in all societies, some people were humane and others were not. Some injured airmen were treated with kindness and compassion. Others were hacked to pieces. It was a lottery. Those who were apprehended by the local police or by military authorities (excluding the SS) were usually treated according to the terms of the Geneva Convention, and this often saved their lives.

It is known that Luftwaffe personnel had a particular respect for RAF bomber crews who had baled out after being shot down by their night fighters, or by flak. This was certainly Reg's experience, as we saw in his own account of his capture. His pilot, George Griffiths, had been mistaken by the Luftwaffe officials who were responsible for him after his capture, for a higher-ranking officer than he actually was. Not being entirely sure of his rank, and anxious to observe the correct protocols, they played safe when they interviewed him, saluting him at regular intervals. He was then taken across Berlin to Spandau prison in a chauffeured limousine: along 'Unter den Linden' and through the Brandenburg Gate, with Luftwaffe personnel pointing out things of interest to him all the way there! Johnny Bushell, Reg's rear gunner, was an NCO, but he was treated with particular kindness and compassion. When he landed, injured, right next to a gun battery, the duty personnel took pity on this poor Englishman, who was in a state of considerable

shock and who had nasty injuries to his face. They fed him and put him
into a warm, comfortable bed to sleep for the night before handing him
over to the authorities for interrogation the next day. The men working
at the gun battery were all youngsters themselves, and they clearly saw
in Johnny Bushell a young man who, like themselves, was just caught
up in a war that he had not started, and in circumstances over which he
had no control.

In his book about Bomber Command, the historian Max Hastings
made this observation: 'Luftwaffe men on the ground in Germany often
showed astonishing fellow-feeling for baled-out RAF crews, saving
them from mobs, and treating them with real kindness.' This implies that
the Lufwaffe crews understood what the RAF crews had been through.
The civilians did not. Neither were the latter bound by military codes of
conduct.

Towards the end of the hostilities, Allied bombing intensified and
the number of civilian casualties climbed steeply. It is known that, at this
point, Nazi officials openly encouraged civilians to take the law into their
own hands if they came across stranded airmen. It had become clear to
the Germans that the Allies were now carrying out 'area bombing', which
involved attacking whole cities, including non-military and non-strategic
targets. The Germans were quite correct in their assumption that this was
a deliberate strategy. In a memorandum issued to command and group
AOCs in the RAF on 12 October 1942, attacks on 'enemy morale' had been
officially sanctioned by the Assistant Chief of Air Staff. Consequently,
there could no longer be any expectation that, if captured, Allied airmen would be afforded the protection of the Geneva Convention. This
would mean that their chances of surviving unscathed after being shot
down were considerably diminished.

In Germany, everything was breaking down at this point and
descending into anarchy. In Britain, most members of the public
supported the idea of a rigorous counter-offensive to break the spirit of
the German people. They felt that, if this would hasten the end of
hostilities, then it could be morally justified. In public, the British
Government, whatever they had sanctioned in private, denied that there
had been a material change in bombing policy. In so doing, they were
fuelling the post-war controversy about the Allied bombing campaign.

Reg's view, which I support, is that area bombing was the lesser of two evils. The greater evil would have been to capitulate and allow the evil Nazi regime to triumph over the Allied offensive.

On 26 October 2005, Reg and Barbara had been treated to a trip in a Cesna light aircraft, to see the eastern side of Berlin from the air, in yet another attempt to 'revisit' the crash site. The pilot, Frank Hellberg, was a delightful man, who treated them with the utmost courtesy and respect. Frank was often engaged in such flights for rich businessmen and tourists, but he offered his services free to Reg and Barbara after Ralf Drescher had told him about the purpose of their visit to Berlin – for they were no ordinary tourists! This is another example of the kindness and friendship that Reg and Barbara experienced in Germany during their various visits there.

The next day, 27 October, at the invitation of the mayor of Köpenick, we attended a meeting with some of those who had replied to Ralf's newspaper appeal for eyewitnesses. This was the last day of our trip to Berlin, as we were booked on a flight back to the UK the following day. At this fascinating and historical conference, stories were shared, friendships were formed, hands were shaken and tears were shed. Many of the Germans present at the reception gave intensely moving accounts of how the bombing of Berlin had affected their families and shaped their lives. They told of heartbreak, destroyed homes, and of personal effects belonging to Allied bomber crews, which had been recovered from smouldering wreckage. One woman witness had in her possession a letter that had been written by a British airman to his beloved, but which had never been delivered. Her late husband, who had been a teenager during the war, had recovered the letter from the wreckage of a Lancaster bomber, and had translated it at the time into German using a small English– German dictionary. While doing this he realised that it was a love letter from a British airman to his sweetheart. Thus stirred in him a strange, primordial understanding that humans are all the same, since Englishmen clearly fall in love and face heartbreak, just as Germans do! The boy was deeply affected by this very personal realisation. As a result of discovering the love letter, he had spent much of his adult life after the war trying to return the letter to the person for whom it had been intended. If he had not had the misfortune to be living in the area of Germany that was to fall under communist control, he might indeed have succeeded in his mission. Details such as this are the little inconsequential stories of war, which never make it into the history books, but which bring history alive and highlight the madness and the tragedy of war, and the seemingly insatiable appetite of the human race for conflict.

Just as the very poignant meeting in Köpenick town hall was drawing to a close, a final witness came forward. His name was Michael Pincus, a retired dentist. He told us of his experience of surviving the bombardment of Berlin and produced an incredible artefact, which changed the whole course of our investigation:

In January 1944, Michael Pincus had been a pupil at a local grammar school. On the morning of 21 January 1944, he had been taking a short cut through the woods to the underground station on his way to school. The previous night he had been incarcerated in a cellar during an air raid that had threatened to destroy his home. Clearly an intelligent and meticulous individual, Pincus had kept a diary throughout the war. In it, he had detailed the precise events of each day, perhaps sensing that he was living through a period of unprecedented historical interest for future generations. Today, a boy of his age with the same gift of foresight would be using social media for this, rather than a personal diary! How easy would it be to lay your hands on a blog entry, one wonders, sixty-two years on? Perhaps we should all still be writing diaries on paper.

Those sixty-two years later, at our meeting in the town hall, Michael Pincus produced the schoolboy diary in which he had written an account of the raid of 20 January 1944. He had subsequently annotated these notes with a drawing of the wreckage of a plane. He had come across the aircraft, which was still smouldering, in the woodland on his way to school the following morning. In his diary entry on the previous evening, he had recorded the time of the impact, and the thoughts of himself and his family, who had been perilously close to the crashed plane, and who had narrowly escaped being buried alive in their own cellar.

Here is my translation into English of his diary entry:

Thursday 20.01 1944 from 1900 hrs. until 2100 hrs. Full alarm/alert.

Heavy attacks on Köpenick and the Elsengrund district as well as the capital itself. We were shaken about in our air-raid shelter. Streams of bombers whistled overhead. The heavy explosions made the ground shake beneath us.

It was time once again to write our wills!

A four-engined Bomber of the Halifax type crashed 200 metres from the Waldburgweg, in the wood, about 100 metres from Hirschgarten Railway Station.

The left wing was broken off about 2/3rds of the way along, and the right hand one about half way along. The fuselage lay flat on the ground. The rear gun turret and lots of ammunition, together with a dead Englishman, lay in the Heidekrugstrasse where they had crashed. Three further young Englishmen lay in the fuselage of the plane.

From the instrument panel of the bomber, I broke off a metal strip which bore the inscription 'SPECIAL TROOP SIGNALLING'.

The wreck of the Bomber was not guarded and the corpses (in the wreck) were not removed until five days later.

Seeing the diary entry, even before I had been able to translate it precisely, was a 'Eureka' moment for everyone present. Reg compared the entry with the known facts about that fateful night, and became convinced that Pincus's sketch and notes referred to his plane, as everything seemed to tie up. This had to be more than a coincidence!

It was tantalising but very frustrating. Pincus had limited English, and we had very little time left before we were due to return to the UK. Nevertheless, Reg was absolutely certain that this was a lead worth following.

Chapter 13

May 2006 – at the Crash Site

After our return to London, Reg relentlessly pursued his inquisition! As a German speaker, I became the go-between, the vital communication link between Michael Pincus and my father. Each time Reg wanted to email Michael Pincus, I would translate his message into German for Michael and then translate Michael's reply back into English for Reg. I felt like the proverbial piggy in the middle. However, bit by bit, we pieced together the facts. But we needed to go back to Germany to continue our research.

As usual, my movements were dictated by the ebb and flow of the demands of an academic year. This is still the case as I write this! In the year 2005–06, the next 'window' when we could all travel to Berlin was the summer half-term holiday at the end of May. We consoled ourselves that it would be warmer by then … although it wasn't!

Claus-Dieter, the museum curator, had wanted Reg to open an exhibition in the local museum in Köpenick. This was about the Allied bombing of Berlin and its effect on the local district. The exhibition's opening was actually delayed until the end of May so that we could take part in it. Sadly, Claus-Dieter's cancer had begun to get the better of him meanwhile, so by the time we arrived for the opening of the exhibition, he was too ill to attend, and the event was hosted by his successor. (Claus-Dieter died six months later, on 4 October 2006.)

Once again our stay was to be a short one, in order to keep the costs manageable. However, as usual, Ralf Drescher had pulled out all the stops to make sure that every minute of our trip was used to the full. During the same day we were due to open the exhibition (in the evening), Ralf had set up a meeting with Michael Pincus and other interested parties. We were to meet in the forest on the edge of Köpenick. The plan was that

Michael would take us into the forest and identify the spot where the crashed plane had been found. It was to be an emotional day. ...

Together with Ralf Drescher, Michael Pincus and his wife Gaby, my parents and me, there was hobby historian Rüdiger Kaddatz, and his wife. Quite a party.

We met up in a small parking area near the entrance to the wood and close to the housing estate in which Michael Pincus had lived as a boy. He pointed out his former house, and also the road where, in June 1933, Hitler's bully boys had massacred twenty-three trade unionist 'trouble-makers' in a week now known as the Blutwoche (blood week). This made an interesting backdrop to the more personal events narrated in Pincus's schoolboy diary.

Shortly after we arrived and everyone had been introduced (or re-introduced), Michael produced a gift-wrapped package and gave it to Reg.

When he had shown us the vital diary entry back in October 2005, a small metal strip had been stuck to the page. The metal fragment bore the words 'Special Troop Signalling'. It had been the first tangible proof that Pincus had really seen a crashed Allied plane in the wood on the morning of 21 January 1944. In 2006, Pincus had removed the metal strip from his diary and then packed it up in a tiny presentation box, such as one might use when giving a piece of jewellery as a present. Inside the presentation box, he had written these words, in his broken English:

Thursday 20.01.1944
At 20.00 about,
Thursday 30.05 2006
At 10.00 about,
In Berlin – Köpenick again.

The thin metal strip had been placed on top of a picture of some roses, probably cut out of a birthday card, bearing the words 'Alles Liebe' (all my love).

This truly was an act of love. Michael Pincus had treasured this small memento for all those years, stuck into his diary and adjacent to the sketch he had made as a teenager. And now he had presented it to Reg!

At the crash site, Pincus produced his schoolboy diary again, minus the metal strip, to show the sketch and report to Rüdiger Kaddatz, who had not seen it previously. The sketch clearly showed the stricken plane and four bodies. Three of these were described as being 'smashed and burned' and still trapped in the aircraft. A fourth body had been flung far away from the main crash site in the wood, and had landed in a nearby street, from which it had been swiftly removed to prevent the incensed civilian population (whose houses had just been bombed) from venting their spleen upon it.

Michael then explained that he had not been able to retrieve any more souvenirs from the plane himself as, the day after discovering the wreck, he had been summoned to attend a compulsory training camp for members of the Hitler Youth, of which membership was obligatory. However, some of his friends had revisited the crash site in the days between the crash and when the plane was finally removed. What a find for a bunch of adolescent boys on their way to school on a grey January morning. How exciting it must have been for them!

After the Hitler Youth camp, Michael Pincus had fled to the Baltic coast with his parents to stay in relative safety at the home of his (Gentile) grandparents. For Pincus was a third generation Jew, and one of his other grandparents was of Jewish origin. By then, the net was closing in on anyone with any Jewish connections whatsoever. The Final Solution was merciless. Because Pincus never saw what had eventually happened to the crashed plane, he had to rely on information from his school mates about this. They had told him that the plane had been broken up by forced labourers, probably Russians, and then it had been removed from the forest. Michael did not know what had become of the four corpses that had been depicted in his sketch – three in the plane and one lying exposed in a nearby street. However, he was aware that a civilian woman had been dragged away from the corpse in the street, as she had been stamping on it and shouting 'Geh' zur Hölle!' (go to hell). This was understandable behaviour in the circumstances, given that this airman had just been bombing her neighbourhood.

I have a vivid recollection of that day in May 2006. It was an unseasonably cold day for the time of year, and a light drizzle was beginning to fall as we entered the wood. But we were undeterred. We walked a little way along a well-trodden path, much used by runners, cyclists and dog walkers. The wood was calm and tranquil, and one could easily see why it is a popular place in which to escape city life for a while. Mingled with the sound of the voices of children on a nature trail, and a few pet dogs barking, was blissful birdsong, with only the occasional rumble of a distant underground train coming into Hirschgarten underground station to remind us that we were on the fringe of a major European capital.

After a while we left the path behind us and veered left into the trees, following Pincus's lead. He did not hesitate or falter. In spite of his advancing years, he was still spritely and sure-footed. He eventually took us into an area where roots and fallen trees made the going more challenging. I have a favourite photograph of Pincus and Reg; two elderly gentlemen who had been on different 'sides' in 1944, now holding hands and steadying each other as they moved along the undulating ground. Then Michael stopped. With his arm extended, he indicated a deep and still visible trench in the undergrowth, which had been hollowed out by the plane's fuselage as it skidded to a halt. We all held our breath and closed our eyes, imagining the horror. To break the tension, half joking I turned to Rüdiger Kaddatz, and said, 'Well, haven't you brought a metal detector?' After what seemed like hesitation, but may not have been, he disappeared back to his van and returned with a detector and a few small tools.

I am not sure about the legality (or otherwise) of what happened next, but happen it did. Rüdi switched on the metal detector and began to sweep the area. It bleeped. We dug. Sometimes, we just found strips of aluminium – which could have been Kit-Kat wrappers, as I remarked jovially at the time! But there was lots of it. Apparently, this was Window – the metal strip that was jettisoned by RAF bombers in an attempt to confuse German radar. I remained unconvinced. Then there were miscellaneous pieces of rusty metal. Could these be Coke cans? However, next came a series of rusty bolts, hinges, brackets and thin pipes. Then bits of what could have been an engine. Then a piece of blackened Perspex, the most significant find yet, as this was curved and blistered, as if it were part of a front- or gun-turret lookout, which had been exposed to intense heat. And then came the jaw-dropping moment. …

For out of the fragrant mass of two and a half generations of decid-
uous leaf mould, came a curved piece of metal with an identification
number stamped rather crudely upon it, and a trade mark, which Rüdiger
Kaddatz was able to identify as that of English Electric (Preston) Ltd. (I
have a strong memory of my mother, Barbara, now eighty-five, wiping
away the mud with a leaf, to expose the number, because we had no other
means of cleaning it up.)

We were totally unprepared for such events. We had nothing at the
ready to contain the fragments we had found. It had simply never occurred
to us that we would find any concrete evidence of an aircraft. We had gone
into the wood with Michel Pincus, on a sort of pilgrimage, to help Reg
find peace, and had not even considered the possibility that we might find
any proof that this was indeed the crash site. As an emergency measure,
we searched in our bags for tissues, plastic carriers, and indeed anything
that would enable us to carry away our findings!

Rüdiger Kaddatz had been involved in other investigations of this
kind, and he knew his onions. If he was excited, then we knew we were
on to something. At the very least, we had found the remains of a crashed
Second World War bomber. We knew that Pincus had identified the plane
that he had seen as a Halifax bomber. And Reg's plane was a Halifax. It
was all coming together. ...

Knowing that we were to attend the opening of the exhibition that
evening, after thanking everyone concerned, we returned to our hotel
to rest in the afternoon. (Investigations of this kind are tiring when you
are in your eighties. And they are still tiring, even if you aren't!)

At least, that was the intention. But we had just not expected this to
happen. Yes, we had known that we would be seeing Pincus again. And
that it had been arranged for us to visit the crash site, and that this would
be an emotional moment. But we had not expected to return to our hotel
with bits of what might be Reg's actual plane!

We knew via Pincus that the plane that had landed in the wood had
remained there under armed guard for a couple of days, to prevent
looting, and that eventually it had been broken up by forced labourers,
who had probably not been too particular about what fell off their carts
when they were taking the plane out of the wood for disposal. Anything

that would have been considered useful to German intelligence would have been removed first, and the bits left behind were just smashed up to facilitate conveyance from the wood. If this were Reg's plane and if Pincus's sketch and verbal account were accurate, there would have been four bodies as well. This tied in with what Reg knew about his crew. Two had baled out (himself and the bomb aimer, Laurie Underwod), one had broken his way out and then parachuted, injured, to the ground (rear gunner, Johnny Bushell), and one, the pilot (George Griffiths) had been miraculously blown out by the explosion. A normal bomber crew consisted of seven members, but Reg's plane had had eight crew-members, as that night they were accompanied by a 'second dickey' pilot, on the sortie to gain operational experience before heading up his own crew. (In this case, however, the poor man was not destined to head his own crew.) The numbers added up. Four POWs. Two killed in action. Two unaccounted for. Eight on board. …

Back at the hotel, Barbara and I tried to have a rest, to prepare ourselves for the evening's events, but Reg just could not keep still. I have a vivid recollection of him standing in the hotel bathroom, using shower gel and a small nailbrush to try to remove sixty-two years' worth of grime and rust from miscellaneous fragments of metal which might have been parts of his plane. He was like a small child at Christmas, full of hope and wonder.

That evening, we attended the very moving opening of the exhibition at the Köpenick museum, at which the story of Reg's quest for his missing plane loomed large. He gave a speech and I translated it, as best as I could, into German, which was tricky as I had no idea beforehand what he was going to say and, in any case, the content of his speech was very much changed in the light of that day's discoveries, although we still had no proof that what we had found was in any way significant. Interesting, certainly, but possibly not significant. We did not dare to hope for any more. I believe that by this point Reg had already achieved a certain degree of the tranquillity he had been seeking for such a very long time. We chatted to locals. We looked at the exhibition. We all exchanged our views on the war and how wonderful it is to live in the era of peace, freedom and relative prosperity that we all enjoy in twenty-first century Europe. And then we went back to our hotel to catch up on the sleep that had so far eluded us that day!

Early the following morning, hobby historian Rüdiger Kaddatz arrived at our hotel. He was extremely animated! He had taken away the fragment with the serial number (a bit like the VIN number on the chassis of a British car) and had some news for us: the fragment was that of a Halifax bomber, Mark II, Series 1A – the same model as Reg's plane! The aircraft had been manufactured by English Electric, in Preston, Lancashire, between August and October 1943. This information narrowed the possible planes down considerably. By comparing the registration numbers of aircraft of the relevant type manufactured at this point in time by English Electric with those known to have crashed on the night of 20/21 January 1944, we were left with just two possibilities. Further research after we returned home to the UK enabled Reg to eliminate the other plane. We really had found Reg's plane, 'Old Flo'! And we were ecstatic – but there was yet more excitement to come. …

Six months later, in November 2006, members of the Berlin police excavated the crash site again, in the presence of MOD and British Embassy officials, at the instigation of the German journalist, Ralf Drescher. This was in order to check for any 'unexploded ammunition'. Ralf had used this ruse to persuade the police to excavate the site using proper equipment, not just a few spades and an amateur metal detector. The investigation had been delayed until the autumn, when the undergrowth would have died down. Fortunately, the Berlin police did not find anything dangerous. However, they did find further fragments of the plane, various tools, part of a parachute harness (printed with instructions in English) and then … human remains. No one had expected this development. After finding the vestiges of the plane, we had been both astonished and delighted. Reg had achieved a feeling of peace at last. There was nothing left to strive for. Or was there?

When planning our visit to the crash site, we had not dared to hope that we would find any tangible evidence of the plane. To discover not just remnants of the aircraft itself, but human remains, elevated the project to a whole new level of importance and poignancy. And it stirred up once again all the emotions associated with the loss of Reg's comrades in such traumatic circumstances.

At first, I regretted this development. How would Reg react to this news? I distinctly remember the night when Ralf Drescher, the journalist, rang me at my home in Farnham, Surrey, to tell me what the police had found that day. It was 1 November 2006, just two days after my husband and I had once more visited Berlin, this time simply as tourists, at Ralf's invitation. Ralf had by now become a firm friend of the family, due to our constant contact by email.

So, on 1 November 2006 I was faced with the task of conveying the news of the fresh discovery to my father, as Ralf's English wasn't up to this. I sat, stunned, by the phone for quite a while after Ralf had rung off. How could I break this revelation to Reg? But tell him I did. In his turn he too sat, stunned, by his telephone. This was no longer about a pile of tangled metal. It was potentially about one of his lost crew, two of whom had never been accounted for. Could these remains be those of Jacky Bremner, the flight engineer, or of Charles Dupueis, the Canadian mid-upper gunner?

The following months were frustrating, as things moved so slowly. At first, the Berlin police would not release the bones, in case they proved to be key evidence in some recent murder investigation or other human tragedy. Their forensic scientists spent some time considering various possibilities, in order to ascertain the probable age of the bones, and to establish how long they had been buried in leaf mould in the woodland.

Eventually, at the end of 2006, having established that the human remains were of an age that would suggest they were linked to the plane crash, the Berlin police handed them over to the British Embassy, who then passed them to the MoD. Reg, who felt that he did not have time on his side, became impatient, and badgered the MoD relentlessly, in order to try to speed things up, and to find out exactly what was going on. But the wheels turn slowly in such cases, as set protocols and procedures must be followed.

Chapter 14

Frustration, then Breakthrough

Once the bones discovered at the crash site had been officially handed over to the British authorities, a chain of events was set in place over which we had no control. The MoD at this point involved the Joint Casualty and Compassionate Centre (JCCC). This organisation provides a casualty and compassionate reporting centre for all the armed forces. It is part of the Service Personnel and Veterans Agency (SPVA) and is based at Innsworth Station in Gloucestershire.

The JCCC wanted to investigate the possibility that the bones found were those of Charles Dupueis, the mid-upper gunner of Reg's plane, who was a French Canadian. Sue Raftree of the JCCC had connections with the Canadian authorities, and arranged to send the bones to Canada, where efforts were being made to trace the family of the late Charles Dupueis. This was early in 2007. Although strenuous efforts were made in Canada, the authorities were unable to find anyone other than distant cousins of the Canadian airman. This was not satisfactory, as mitochondrial DNA testing is usually used to establish identity when the mother or immediate siblings of the deceased can be found. Obviously, in this case, because of the time that had elapsed, we were only looking for any siblings of the deceased who were born of the same biological mother (who would have died some time ago) or indeed of their descendants in the maternal line.

To complicate matters further, there were funding issues in Canada, which not only impeded the progress of the investigation, but also meant that a considerable amount of time was wasted while the relevant authorities argued about who was going to pay for it all. In the end, it was concluded that no really useful information had been found, and so the bones were returned to the UK. By this time, it was early 2008. This meant that a whole year had elapsed while the bones were in Canada. Reg was enormously frustrated by the lack of activity during this period.

Ralf Drescher, as an investigative journalist, does not let the grass grow under his feet! While nothing much was happening, Ralf took it upon himself to try to find the pilot who had shot down Reg's plane in 1944.

Hauptmann Leopold Fellerer had been an Austrian airman flying with the Luftwaffe. We had discovered that he had been awarded the Knight's Cross (das Ritterkreuz) and that he had been considered an ace night-fighter aviator with an amazing track record of success in shooting down enemy planes. We also knew that he had continued to work as a pilot after the war. However, surfing the net, Ralf had discovered that Fellerer had perished in a tragic aircraft accident in the 1960s, which was thought to have been caused by mechanical failure rather than pilot error. Was this to be the end of Ralf's investigation? Absolutely not! Ralf continued his research, by trying to find living relatives of the pilot. And find them he did.

The tenacious Ralf located Fellerer's grandson, Stefan Salem, who was living in Tülln, the town on the Danube where his grandfather had lived. It turned out that Stefan was an important member of the local Scout Association in Austria. Through this connection, Ralf had made contact with Stefan by email, and Stefan, intrigued by the story, had exchanged several emails with Ralf before Ralf eventually put him in touch with me.

We corresponded amicably by email, comparing notes about our links with the international family of Scouting. Then it transpired that Stefan and his girlfriend would be visiting Gilwell Park in Essex (very close to my parents' Chigwell home) in August 2007, for the celebration of the centenary of the Scouting movement. It was an opportunity too good to miss! With Reg's agreement and encouragement, I invited Stefan and his girlfriend to visit us in Essex during his stay, to meet us and to exchange stories.

To our surprise and delight, Stefan and his girlfriend accepted my invitation. When they were in Essex, I contacted Stefan by mobile phone, and we agreed that I would meet him at the local Central Line tube station. How would he recognise me, he had asked? Instead of sending him a photograph, I simply said: 'When you come out of the tube station, I will be wearing my son's international Scout scarf. You will then know who I am!' This had a figurative as well as a literal meaning, both in German (which I had used to communicate with him) and in English. For the Scout scarf, an international sign of friendship and equality, was the perfect ice-breaker in this potentially delicate situation.

We met. We shook hands, using the left handshake of the international Scout and Guide community. I took Stefan and his partner back to my parents' home in Chigwell, Essex, and from there to a lovely country pub, where we had a wonderful lunch, at Reg's invitation. After lunch, we sat in the sun and drank champagne in Reg's garden. I have not seen Stefan since, although we are connected on Facebook. Just meeting him and his wife-to-be on that one occasion was a magical experience, and one that I will treasure forever. It proved to be an emotional and unique occasion, which made up for the lack of progress on the identification of the bones. It was a beautiful August day, during which bridges were built and tears were shed. Once more, I was reminded of the hideous pointlessness of conflict, of the joys of living in peacetime, and of the value of meaningful friendship between nations.

In the meantime, during the long period of inactivity and lack of news from Canada, Reg had decided to take the law into his own hands, as he felt that time was running out for him. Among his POW notes and letters, he had in his possession a poignant and tragic letter, which had been sent to his mother, my grandmother, on 14 February 1944. It was from Ada Bremner, the mother of Reg's flight engineer, who lived in Newcastle upon Tyne. It said: 'I hope that soon our minds will be at rest through our hearing good news, either from our sons themselves or from the Air Ministry. Should you receive news of the whereabouts of your boy, would you be so kind as to inform me. I would be most grateful. In the meantime, I hope that all is well with each one of them.'

Using this letter as a starting point for his investigation, Reg wrote a speculative email to the *Newcastle Chronicle*, trying to enlist their help with his search. He explained the outcome of his hunt for the missing plane, the fact that human remains had been found, and that two of his crew had never been accounted for, one of these being John Bremner, his flight engineer, and the other, a Canadian named Charles Dupueis.

After several letters, phone calls and emails to the newspaper, an article was finally published on 17 April 2007. Luckily, the article was seen by a distant cousin of John Bremner (known as Jack, or Jacky to his family). However, the cousin did not, as requested, respond to the newspaper in the first instance, but instead contacted Marjorie Acon, Bremner's surviving sister, directly. Regrettably, he did not break the news gently or diplomatically and, in so doing, upset the elderly Mrs Acon, who then involved her daughter, Lesley, and son-in-law, Paul Fallon. Paul contacted the newspaper and explained that the news had been broken in an insensitive way, and asked if he could be put in touch with Reg! This led to a very long and convoluted telephone call, during which Reg explained everything clearly. Now that he was in possession of the full facts, Paul proved to be really keen to get involved and help Reg, together with the MoD, to solve the mystery.

After she had recovered from the initial shock, Marjorie Acon, John Bremner's sister, also became enthusiastic about the discovery. For nearly sixty-four years, she had not known what had happened to her late brother, who had never returned from the war, who was recorded as unaccounted for, and whose name was listed on the Runnymede Memorial as MIA (missing in action). Marjorie and her family had never been able to find peace after losing Jacky, whose whereabouts and fate were hitherto unknown. Now all that could change, and this was a very exciting prospect for the elderly lady.

So in January 2008, representatives from the JCCC visited Marjorie, offering her compassion and moral support, before asking her if she would be willing to undergo DNA testing in order to establish whether the remains found were indeed those of her late brother, or of the Canadian, Charles Dupueis. Marjorie agreed. In April, the results of the mitochondrial DNA testing established a definitive match between the remains found at the crash site and Marjorie Acon. She was eighty-eight years of age. For sixty-four years she had not known what had happened to her younger brother, and the news stirred, quite understandably, a range of mixed but nonetheless powerful emotions in her. They had finally found her brother. At last, she would have an opportunity to find peace.

I can still remember that day in April 2008 when I heard the news that the JCCC had proved that the human remains that had been found as a result of my efforts and those of Reg, were indeed those of Jacky Bremner. I was sitting in a classroom in Witley, Surrey, serving out my notice in a school that had recently announced its intention to make me redundant at the end of that academic year, due to over-staffing and falling pupil numbers. It was a teaching job I had loved, and so the prospect of losing it had made me quite depressed and demotivated, since I had just turned fifty years of age. This fact, together with the price tag that goes with my long experience as a modern languages teacher, would make it difficult for me to find another permanent teaching job.

I was supervising a class who were doing a test in exam conditions. Because of this, I was working on my computer, and I had made use of the gained time to have a look at my emails. Surprisingly, as this was my work email account, and not my private one, there was an email from Reg. This worried me, as he would normally only contact me at work in the case of a genuine emergency. Nothing in the subject line gave me any idea what the email was about. So I opened it.

The email stated quite simply: 'It was Bremner.' I needed no further explanation! I shot out of my chair, unable to contain my emotion. The announcement put my recent news concerning my redundancy, into some perspective. This was an amazing development! Suddenly, my redundancy seemed unimportant, as I realised that I had done far more meaningful things with my knowledge of German than try and teach it to reluctant teenagers!

I could not wait to talk to Reg and find out more. When we spoke, he revealed that Marjorie Acon, Bremner's sister, had been informed by the JCCC of the results the previous day. Since Reg's efforts had been so instrumental in all that had unfolded, the MoD/JCCC had seen fit to inform Reg of the outcome, after notifying Bremner's immediate family. Straight away, I contacted Ralf Drescher, whose efforts had led to this amazing discovery. He was overwhelmed with emotion, and has since told my daughter, on her recent trip to Berlin, that publishing Reg's story and being involved with its aftermath was the best thing that had ever happened to him during his career as a journalist!

The JCCC, part of the Service Personnel and Veterans Agency, is based at Innsworth in Gloucestershire. This is the branch of the MoD that was charged with conveying the news of the successful DNA match to Marjorie and her family, and ultimately for the organisation of John Bremner's burial. As a member of the armed forces killed in action, John was entitled to be buried with full military honours, but these things cannot be arranged overnight. His burial site was to be in the British and Commonwealth war cemetery in Berlin. It had, by now, been sixty-four years since he was killed in action over the city.

The site of the Berlin 1939–45 War Cemetery was selected by the British Occupation Authorities and Commission officials jointly in 1945, soon after hostilities ceased. Graves were brought to the cemetery from the Berlin area and from other parts of eastern Germany. The great majority of those buried there, approximately 80% of the total, were airmen who were lost in the air raids over Berlin and other towns in eastern Germany. The remainder were men who died as prisoners of war, some of them in the forced march westwards from camps in Poland as the Eastern Front began to crumble.

The cemetery contains 3,595 Commonwealth graves of the Second World War, 397 of them unidentified. Among the graves that Reg had already located in this cemetery were those of the two deceased members of his crew who had been formally identified in 1944: Eric Church, the wireless operator, and Kenneth Stanbridge, the second dickey pilot, who was Australian. Bremner's burial at the site would mean that three of the four members of Reg's crew who were killed in action on the night of 20 January 1944 would be buried in the same cemetery. It is, of course, possible that the fourth crew member, whose remains are still unaccounted for (the Canadian mid-upper gunner, Charles Dupueis), is buried there too, but in one of the unmarked graves. If the bodies were, as Michael Pincus put it, 'completely smashed and burned', then it is feasible that Dupueis's body was retrieved from the wreckage, but that it was in such a poor state that it could not be identified.

Reg's research had enabled him to establish that both Eric Church's body and that of Kenneth Stanbridge were relocated at the Berlin cemetery after the war, in 1947, having been removed from the temporary graves where they were first interred. It is known that Stanbridge's body was transferred from a temporary military grave at Döberitz, in western Berlin, which was also the site of a POW camp. It is also established that Church's body had previously been interred in a German civilian cemetery in Fürstenwalde, a town 55 kilometres to the east of Berlin. Initially, the reasons for this had been a mystery to Reg, but it later transpired that Church's body had been removed first from the scene, as his was the one that had landed in a street in the middle of a residential area, away from the wrecked plane in the wood, and it had consequently been removed in a hurry and buried, probably without ceremony, in the first available grave. Stanbridge's body (and maybe those of the other deceased crewmembers), was almost certainly taken from the wreckage several days later, and in less chaotic circumstances, and so it had been possible to follow proper protocols and bury him in a military cemetery.

While in captivity, Reg's pilot, George Griffiths, had been asked by his interrogators: 'Tell us the name of your wireless operator, so that we can bury him with a name.' This is why Church's body, although buried initially in a distant grave, had actually been properly labelled. Stanbridge, and probably the other body or bodies, or what was left of them, were sent to Döberitz. Of these, only Kenneth Stanbridge was formally identified, and so his name appeared on his tombstone when he was finally laid to rest in Charlottenburg in 1947. We know that once the Charlottenburg cemetery had been established, where possible the MoD buried whole crews in consecutive graves, if they had all been found in one location. Interestingly, next to Stanbridge's resting place is a series of unmarked graves. It is possible that one of these is that of the Canadian, Charles Dupueis, but this we will never know. It is also feasible that some of Jacky Bremner's remains are in one of the other unmarked graves, or even that there are the remains of more than one airman in any one of the graves. Such gravestones are marked, as is the custom, with the words 'Known unto God'.

The remains of Jacky Bremner that were unearthed in 2006 were not complete, but they had been unequivocally identified as his remains, as a result of the mitochondrial DNA testing, which had cross-matched them with the profile of his sister Marjorie. The scientific knowledge required to perform this kind of testing is relatively new, and so it could not have been used when burying the remains of airmen in the period immediately after the war. Tragic though it is, it is true to say that the delayed finding of Jacky Bremner's remains in November 2006 enabled him to be identified in a way that would not have been possible even twenty years earlier, as such testing was still in its infancy until the early 1990s. It should also be noted that the wood in Köpenick where Jacky Bremner's remains were found was effectively behind the Iron Curtain until 1989, which would have seriously inhibited any attempt to find the truth.

The detailed information Reg had obtained about the original graves of Kenneth Stanbridge and Eric Church had informed the questions he had asked the eyewitness, Michael Pincus, via our email contact with him in the winter and spring of 2005/06. A full year elapsed between our first encounter with Michael Pincus and the day on which the Berlin police unearthed Bremner's remains. It is now clear that Church's body is separated from Stanbridge's in the graveyard because, although they were members of the same crew, they were not found together. The chaos in Berlin in 1944 had prevented such niceties as trying to keep the remains of deceased RAF airmen together in crews once they had been separated. Our whole situation was like a giant jigsaw puzzle with millions of pieces, which we slowly put in place. Were these findings a happy coincidence? To be sure, they were a fitting reward for Reg's patience and persistence, but so much could have gone wrong! Just one missing link would have prevented us from achieving the final incredible outcome. But achieve it we did.

As I remarked in the prologue to this book, the truth is often stranger than fiction. Reg is not, and never has been, a religious man, but one day when we were discussing his story for the umpteenth time, he said: 'This was greater than any of us. Someone, somewhere, has made this happen!' And I could not argue with that.

Chapter 15

Pocklington 2008

In the UK, there is still at least one airworthy Lancaster, which is regularly showcased during military fly-pasts, and sometimes at air shows. Everyone has heard of the Lancaster bomber! Together with the Spitfire, it is up on a pedestal, as an icon of the Second World War. There is a 'rescued' Halifax bomber on show in a hangar at the National Air Force Museum of Canada at CFB Trenton, near Kingston, Ontario. But there is only one Halifax bomber left in the UK, and it cannot fly! This is because, after the war, the Halifax bombers were all broken up and 'recycled'. No one had the foresight to realise that, like the more famous Lancaster bombers, they were of immense historical importance. That is, until relatively recently.

Staff at the Yorkshire Air Museum at Elvington, near York, were determined to put this right, and set about the task of creating a lasting memorial to the Halifax bomber. They felt that the museum, being located on a former Second World War air base from which Halifax bombers had been flown, should have a Halifax bomber as its centrepiece, but none had survived the scrapping of these important aircraft. A staff member of the Elvington museum, commented: 'A commemorative museum to the Allied air forces without a Halifax would be like a frame without a picture.' Thus began a project involving years of painstaking work by a dedicated team of volunteers, who decided to build their own Halifax with as many original parts as possible.

They had located the first piece by chance when they heard of a derelict section of Halifax fuselage that was being used as a hen coop by a farmer on the Isle of Lewis! The farmer had bought it after the war, when aircraft based at Stornoway had been scrapped. By the 1980s it had half sunk into a peat bog. So they organised a JCB and asked the RAF to come to the rescue, which they did by sending a helicopter to help with the salvage operation. Drivers volunteered to collect the large piece of airframe. Then came the huge task of gathering the hundreds, if not thousands, of bits they would need to faithfully reproduce a facsimile of the bomber. And the project needed lots of willing helpers.

'People just came out of the woodwork,' said a staff member. 'It was amazing; we had everyone from doctors to architects and civil engineers. All were skilled men and it was marvellous.' More help arrived when British Aerospace apprentices manufactured the fuselage as part of their training course. And once word got out, their phone kept ringing as people who had dug up pieces of crashed Halifaxes in France and Germany offered to send them to Yorkshire.

The team had already had a stroke of luck when the original plans turned up. Handley Page had gone into liquidation many years beforehand, and most of its documents had been incinerated. But critically, one employee had saved the Halifax drafts and had sent them to the Imperial War Museum in Duxford. The same former Handley Page employee had passed this information on to them when he first heard about the Elvington project.

The aircraft took twelve years to build, mostly from scratch, and appropriately enough the bomber – christened 'Friday the 13th' – was rolled out on Friday 13 September 1996. It was named after the most illustrious Halifax to have flown with Bomber Command, one that flew 128 successful missions with 158 Squadron, from Lissett in East Yorkshire. After the war, it suffered the ignominy of being dismantled for scrap.

'Because of all the volunteers, the Halifax actually cost very little to make and the day it rolled out was really thrilling,' said the museum. 'The queue of cars went all the way to Grimston Bar and down the A64. There were VIPs, people who came from all over, and of course there were the veterans. Many of them were in tears as they got the chance, once again, to sit in the cockpit of a Halifax bomber. Since then, I think it's given a lot of pleasure to many people.'

One of the people to whom the reconstructed Halifax bomber gave enormous pleasure was Reg, who first visited it before it was completed. He was enthralled by the prospect of being able to go inside the fuselage once more and relive his most poignant memories. Such was his missionary zeal, that he was not only determined to see the reconstructed aircraft for himself, but he was also keen that his own family should share in the experience of a 'guided tour' of the bomber, given by himself, while he was still fit enough to do this.

So it was that, in August 2008, just three months before we buried Reg's long-lost comrade, we travelled to Elvington for this emotional and informative visit. Reg had contacted the museum ahead of time to request access to the interior of the Halifax, which has to be booked in advance. Originally included in the trip were my parents, my husband David and our son Chris. We had arranged to meet up at the museum with Laurie Underwood, Reg's bomb aimer, and members of his family, including some of his grandchildren. Paul Fallon was also present, with his wife Lesley. Lesley Fallon is the niece of John Bremner, the flight engineer who was due to be buried in Berlin two months later. It was quite a party! Members of my family (five of us) decided to travel from my parents' home in Essex to Elvington in our Vauxhall Zafira, which was already going to be quite a squeeze. And that was before I mentioned the proposed visit to Ralf Drescher, the German journalist, who had 'made it all happen'. Ralf wistfully expressed his regret that he would not be there to witness the emotional reunion of man and plane. Feeling that Ralf's presence would somehow make the visit complete, I rashly invited him to come over! So Ralf quickly booked himself on a flight to Stansted and he joined us for the trip. It was very cosy with six adults in the Zafira (although it could, theoretically, seat seven), but it was worth the effort. Ralf's presence added extra poignancy to the occasion, and he was able to make an emotional photo and video record of the event for posterity.

Watching Reg's reaction's inside the plane brought tears to my eyes and a lump to my throat. It seemed incredible that this now elderly man had once risked his life as a navigator, crammed into such a small, freezing space, and with the awesome responsibility of guiding his crew to their destination and back again. It was fascinating to see how well he remembered where everything had been situated. He was twenty again, and definitely 'back in the zone'. This was in spite of the sixty-four years and seven months that had elapsed since that last fateful mission in his Halifax, LW337, or 'Old Flo', as she was fondly known to her crew. I have an abiding memory of Reg acting out his part as navigator at his little fold-up table, and of the late Laurie Underwood, Reg's bomb aimer, who was also demonstrating his role, prone and facing forwards, just as he would have been when aiming the bombs back on that night.

The visit was followed by a photo call and then tea in the former NAAFI, which gave us a chance to share news and catch up. It was a day of reminiscences, but also one when we all looked forward to the event that would take place in Berlin that October.

However, it wasn't over yet, for as we left the museum in the unseasonable drizzle, I saw a signpost that informed us that we were a mere 8 miles from Pocklington, where Reg's 102 Squadron had been based. I said: 'Let's go and see it!' This time, it was Reg who seemed lukewarm about the idea, but I wasn't going to be fobbed off with a lack of enthusiasm now that we were so near to his former air base. Reg was overruled.

After a couple of false turns, and asking passers-by, we located the former home of 102 Squadron. A small sign at the entrance announced that the site was now the home of the Wolds Gliding Club. Reg started to protest again, but we followed the muddy track up to the clubhouse, parked the car, and got out. We did not feel that we were trespassing, because near the clubhouse there was a modest memorial to the lost airmen of 102 Squadron. After paying our respects at this little memorial, we turned our attention to the clubhouse. In those days, mum was fitter and more adventurous than she has since become, and with her northern-born lack of reserve (she is so unlike Reg in that respect), she charged into the clubhouse bar and told the assembled members that her husband had taken off from Pocklington in January 1944 and had never returned – until now! Predictably, we were invited into the clubhouse, where we received a warm welcome and were requested to sign the visitors' book. Reg was so emotional by this point that he had to ask me to remind him of the number of his Halifax bomber, because he had temporarily forgotten it in the highly charged atmosphere of the moment.

We spent a couple of hours telling our story to the gliding enthusiasts, and then came the great surprise! One of the club members, Tony Kendall, announced: 'The weather looks OK tomorrow.' And then, addressing his remark directly to Reg, he said: 'How do you fancy going up in a glider so you can relive that last take-off? Hopefully, you'll come back safely this time!' To our absolute astonishment, Reg agreed, almost without hesitation!

So, the next day we returned to Pocklington, where Reg had to sign lots of disclaimers before he was allowed to fly. Barbara looked very apprehensive as he eagerly put his signature to various official documents. He had previously been asked: 'Do you want to go up in a proper vintage wooden glider or a modern fibre-glass type?' It had been clear from the tone of Tony's question that the vintage machine was considered to have more style and character, not to mention an illustrious history. For Reg, there was no contest. It had to be the wooden glider. Previous passengers had included HRH Prince Philip. (This was interesting, as Reg was to make another connection with the Duke of Edinburgh in July 2009, but more about that in due course.)

When Reg was strapped into the tiny passenger seat of the glider, he once again morphed into a twenty-year-old airman on a mission, going through the well-rehearsed safety routines that had helped to save his life nearly sixty-five years previously. He examined the safety straps fastened around his torso, and immediately asked: 'How do I get out of this thing, and where's the ripcord?' Yes, at the age of eighty-five years and seven months, he once again had a parachute strapped to his back! It was incredible. We all prayed that he wouldn't need to use it on this occasion. ...

The glider was towed off the runway into the air by a light aircraft, and then the cable was released, and the glider continued its journey using only the power of the wind and air currents for propulsion. In spite of the good forecast, there had been some light rain, and at one point the glider disappeared into a huge black cloud. We all held our breath. Barbara turned green. And then the glider emerged from the cloud, cruised, turned, and landed safely some minutes later. It had been quite an adventure, and fairly bumpy by all accounts. Reg had been thrilled by the chance to fly over Pocklington again, but I know that he was glad when the glider landed without incident. 'This time, I made it!' he quipped.

Tony Kendall had given Reg another memorable experience, bringing him one step further to achieving a sense of resolution. Our trips to the Yorkshire wartime airfields of 4 Group at Pocklington and Elvington were drawing to a close. After a pub lunch, we made our way down the M1, to the south, and home. The events of 16 October, a few weeks later, would complete that sense of enduring peace.

Chapter 16

Back to Berlin

The logistics of organising Jacky Bremner's funeral more than sixty-four years after his death were monumentally complicated. At this point, I would like to pay tribute to the sterling work of JCCC member Sue Raftree, who masterminded the whole occasion. Sue had had to explain the complexities of organising such an event to Reg at the time, so that he could understand why so much time would elapse between the finding of the human remains, and the date of the ceremony.

Since the Queen's Colour Squadron was to be involved, along with a large number of dignitaries and relatives, the date for the funeral, 16 October 2008, was not set until the beginning of that year. Preparations for a military funeral had, in fact, been in progress even before it had been established that the human remains found at the crash site were definitely those of Jacky Bremner. The MoD had also had to work closely with the British Embassy in Berlin to make the arrangements.

The whereabouts of Reg and Jacky Bremner's families were obviously already known to the MoD. In addition, Reg was able to provide details of the pilot's widow (George Griffiths had died in 1998), of the rear gunner, Johnny Bushell, and of the bomb aimer, Laurie Underwood, since the four men had kept loosely in touch since the war, and had indeed assembled again in 1994 to commemorate the fiftieth anniversary of their miraculous escape.

That left Kenneth Stanbridge, the Australian second dickey pilot, Eric Church, the wireless operator, and the Canadian mid-upper gunner, Charles Dupueis. Attempts to find close relatives of the Canadian had ceased in early 2008, when the research in Canada was abandoned and the remains, which at that stage were still unidentified, were returned to the UK.

Strenuous endeavours by the MoD finally traced Kenneth Stanbridge's daughter, who had been born in August 1944, seven months after her father went missing. Similar undertakings were made to trace Eric Church's relatives in the UK, including appeals on the radio and in the press, but these attempts had initially borne no fruit.

Once the date of the funeral and approximate numbers had been established, Sue Raftree of the MoD's JCCC had arranged flights (with British Airways from Heathrow) for the veterans, their immediate relatives, and various military dignitaries and participants, who were all to be flown out to Berlin at the MoD's expense, and who would be staying together in the same hotel. Other relatives of crewmembers (including myself and my siblings, Robert and Helen) would follow, having made their own travel and accommodation arrangements.

Incredibly, just a few days before the main party left for Berlin, Eric Church's son, Michael, was traced to an address in the New Forest. Michael had had no idea about his father's story, having simply grown up knowing that his father had been lost in action in the Second World War. Like Bernice de Heaume, Kenneth Stanbridge's daughter, Michael had been born seven months after his father's death, in August 1944. Michael was finally found at such a late stage in the proceedings that one of the JCCC members kindly gave up her place on the (now full) British Airways flight to Berlin so that Michael and his partner could attend Jacky Bremner's funeral. Like Bernice de Heaume, Michael Church would be visiting his father's grave for the first time. And, intriguingly, and poignantly for Reg, Michael was the 'baby' mentioned in Chapter 4.

This would mean that the Canadian, Charles Dupueis, would be one of only two members of the crew of LW337 who would not have a blood relative at the funeral. Instead, he was represented by a member of the Canadian Embassy staff. Laurie Underwood, the bomb aimer, who lived in Yorkshire, was aware of the arrangements, but was sadly too frail to attend the funeral. In spite of this, I think it truly amazing, and a great tribute to Sue Raftree and her staff at the JCCC, that four out of the eight crewmembers were represented by their relatives, and two of them (Reg and Johnny Bushell) were there in person to pay their respects to Jacky Bremner as he made his final journey to his place of rest. It was awe-inspiring.

On the day before the funeral, Wednesday 15 October, there would be a press conference at the British Embassy in Berlin, a superb edifice designed by the acclaimed British architect, Michael Wilford. The building, which was opened in the year 2000, having replaced an earlier embassy, has an imaginative futuristic design, which makes good use of both the available space and of natural light. It proved to be a motivational and uplifting venue for our press conference, and I felt that it was a great privilege to be invited there.

Sue Raftree had organised for contemporary photographs of the eight crewmembers of LW337 ('Old Flo') to be projected on a giant screen during the proceedings. One of these photographs, a superb portrait of Jacky Bremner in uniform, had only been discovered after having been hidden at the back of a wardrobe for many years, when Marjorie Acon, Bremner's sister, was preparing to fly out to his funeral. It had also been emailed to Reg just as he was being interviewed by ITN's Jon Gilbert, and Jon was delighted that I had been able to forward a copy of the picture in time for the ITN news coverage as well.

When Mrs Acon, Jacky Bremner's sister, was interviewed by the media at the press conference in Berlin, on the eve of her brother's funeral, she gave a moving account of how much she had loved her younger brother and how glad she was that he was finally being laid to rest in her presence, something she had only ever been able to dream about.

Thursday 16 October, the morning of the funeral, dawned grey and cloudy, with a light drizzle over Berlin. Reg was whisked away early from the hotel to be interviewed for the Radio 4 *Today* programme, and I was contemplating the skies and wondering which coat to wear. Miraculously, while we were having breakfast, the skies began to clear and glow. By the time we left the hotel, the sun was struggling with the clouds, and winning. It was turning into one of those crisp autumn days, reminiscent of a now distant summer: tinged with mellow, golden sunlight, but with just enough of a chill in the air to remind us of the impending winter; bitter-sweet. It was as though the weather had sensed the contradictory emotions that were to be displayed later that day, and wanted to play its part in creating the right atmosphere for the occasion.

We boarded a British Embassy coach and headed for the Anglican church in which Bremner's memorial service was to be held. Sue Raftree had arranged for a Northumbrian piper to 'play in' the coffin when it arrived, but in the end Jacky Bremner's family decided that this would be just too heartfelt a reminder of Jacky's Northumbrian origins, and the piper didn't perform.

The occasion was overwhelmingly emotional. I can't ever remember being so moved by a funeral. The fact that Jacky had been dead for nearly sixty-five years did nothing to diminish the poignancy of seeing his coffin, draped with the Union flag, borne into the little church by the RAF pall-bearers; beautiful, youthful young men, who had been born long after Britain had recovered from the war, and when it had prospered again. Nevertheless, their immaculate uniforms and serious, handsome faces were a stark reminder, not just of the young Jacky Bremner, but of each and every one of the 55,573 honourable and courageous young airmen of Bomber Command, the cream of our nation's youth, who gave their lives to secure our freedom. They fell from the skies just as they reached the threshold of their adult lives. Such a waste. ... As Noel Coward observed in his touching poem, 'Lie in the Dark and Listen', they had been players in a tense and tragic drama, while many others of their age had been able to lead relatively normal lives, because of their reserved occupations, or because of their status in society, or just because luck was on their side.

Although Bremner's funeral service was harrowing, it was also gloriously uplifting. Paul Fallon, Marjorie Acon's son-in-law, gave this most moving address to those assembled:

Eulogy for Sergeant John Bremner (born 11th January 1922, in Elswick, Newcastle upon Tyne; died 20th January 1944, over Hirschgarten Friedrichshagen, Berlin). Delivered at St George's Anglican Episcopal Church, Neu-Westend, 14052, Berlin, by Paul Fallon on 16th October 2008

Reverend Ahrens, Reverend Dr Richardson, Ladies and Gentlemen,

Marjorie Acon, Sergeant John Bremner's sister, has asked me to share with you her sentiments about her younger brother, whom she knew as Jacky, and whose short life, that ended so long ago, we commemorate today. Others here have spoken of his three comrades who fell in

Berlin on the same day.

She recalls Jacky as a gentle, and yet strong person, with a lovable personality. His empathy for others was legendary – at the age of 12 he brought home two street urchins, asking his parents to attend to their needs. This meant his mother having to make clothes to kit them out as well as raid her pantry of rationed food. A love of animals was his passion too – he was forever rescuing stray cats, dogs and birds. But like all the Bremners, he was practical and skilled.

In 1936, John Bremner was apprenticed as a joiner to his uncle and became a craftsman. Marjorie recalls a brother with unstoppable enthusiasm and determination. Both his mother and his age were barriers to his joining the Royal Air Force, but his quiet, unswerving drive brought him the only thing he wanted to do – to serve on operational flying duties. And so it was that he joined Bomber Command's aircrew as a Flight Engineer with 102 Squadron at RAF Pocklington on 8th December 1943.

Mrs Acon wants to say how appreciative she is today – and how much her mother (who refused to believe to her dying day that Jacky had been lost) would have been too – to see Jacky honoured in this way in the presence of his former aircrew colleagues and their families, and by his country. Reg Wilson and John Bushell, who flew with Jacky on his final mission, are here now.

In February 1944, Jacky's mother wrote to Reg's mother, some three weeks after Halifax LW337 ('Old Flo') went down over Berlin. Both women were waiting for news of their sons, and apart from extending sympathy to Mrs Wilson, Mrs Bremner proposed that they both stay on the case in pursuit of their sons. Reg, Old Flo's Navigator, is not only here in person today, but it is because of his determination that we are all commemorating Sergeant Bremner. Reg eventually delivered on the two families' covenant by finding Old Flo, and hence Jacky. What, after all, is a navigator if he is not someone who guides his crew to their final destination?

Thank you.

Paul Fallon

Reg was immensely moved by Paul Fallon's address. The analogy that Paul made between what Reg had achieved between July 2005 and October 2008, and the duties of a navigator to guide his crew out on a mission, and then to guide them safely home again, was truly inspired, and was the only thanks Reg had ever needed for the research he had done.

After the church service, the funeral party moved on to the military cemetery. This was followed by a traditional burial service, with the laying of wreaths, a bugler playing the last post, and the Queen's Colour Squadron officiating.

John Bremner's tombstone bore the following inscription:

> They travelled a while
> Towards the sun
> And left the vivid air
> Signed with their honour.

These words were chosen by John's sister, Marjorie, who wished his epitaph to refer not just to his sacrifice, but to the collective sacrifices made by the whole crew of LW337.

Following the funeral, there was a reception at a restaurant, where Marjorie was presented with a box containing the wartime medals to which her brother had been entitled, but which had never been claimed by his relatives after his death. Then Ralf Drescher gave Marjorie the clasp from her brother's parachute, which had been found with his remains in November 2006. She was deeply touched and, once again, moved to tears. Then she brightened up and cheerfully announced: 'I'll keep them with my best china!'

Later that day, members of the funeral party visited the crash site, where Ralf had erected a small, hand-made memorial to mark the spot in the woodland where Jacky Bremner had been found. An RAF chaplain said prayers. Birds sang. We laid flowers once again, this time on the spot where Jacky's remains had been found, rather than his final, official resting place.

And so we are back to where our story began: 'Beneath the gentle autumn sun …' intoned the television presenter, as he described the deeply moving scene that was unfolding before him. Barbara Wilson, then seventy-eight years old, turned to me, her elder daughter Janet, and with her eyes full of wonder and glistening with emotion, softly breathed these words: 'Just think, your father started all this!'

Reg certainly had started it. Without his efforts, John Bremner's remains would never have been found. His family might never have found peace. John's sister, Marjorie Acon, was a frail eighty-eight years old when she finally saw her brother laid to rest, nearly sixty-five years after his death. She died three months later, in January 2009, just after her own eighty-ninth birthday. But she died peacefully, no longer haunted by the memory of her younger brother's disappearance in wartime. To quote her own words, she had been 'spared long enough to lay my brother to rest'.

Chapter 17

Catharsis, Reconciliation and Closure

During my childhood, my father often seemed distant and preoccupied. At that time we did not have a warm and close relationship, such as we do today, and things were often strained between us. My upbringing was most certainly influenced by my father's pessimistic and risk-adverse nature. Dad did not want to talk about the war, or its aftermath, either on a personal or a political level. Like many others of his generation, he just got on with his life. This state of affairs made it all the more surprising to me when he did finally start to open up. However, even after this happened, there were certain questions that I felt I could not ask him.

The controversial bombing of Dresden was discussed in the media from time to time, and I knew that this was a subject that aroused passionate feelings in my father. Although he had not taken part in the raid, as he had been a prisoner for twelve months by the time it happened, I knew this subject was a no-go area, and so I avoided it.

But, once my father had propelled himself into the limelight by actively seeking the crash site, controversial questions were often put to him by journalists, both here and in Germany. This forced him to analyse his feelings so that he could answer questions honestly and directly without becoming visibly troubled. I think he had to work on his technique for quite some time. In the end, he became quite adept at being interviewed by the media, and his later interviews are far more coherent than the early ones, and therefore far more informative.

Dad had joined the RAF in 1941 because he wanted to fly a Spitfire over London and defend it from German bombs. First and foremost, he wanted to defend his country from evil and fight in the cause of freedom and justice. Historian Max Hastings accurately described people like my father who, having volunteered for the RAF in the hope of flying Spitfires, had ended up in Bomber Command. He referred to them as 'romantic young idealists, almost to a man aspiring fighter pilots'. He also described these brave young men as 'the most highly trained front-line fighters in the history of warfare'. Hastings had particular praise for Bomber Command pilots and navigators who, according to him 'represented the highest skills – most of the latter (navigators) had been eliminated from pilot training courses'. This was the case for my father. Being a navigator was definitely second best. In either case, according to Max Hastings, Bomber Command navigators and pilots were the 'élite of the élite' both in terms of their intellect and their skills.

But they were also human, and therefore fallible. They flew at night, going against the natural biorhythms of the body. Research has shown that the body and the psyche are at their most vulnerable at night. And yet this was when these young men were put to the ultimate test. It is known that those who do any kind of shift work, or who experience jet lag on a regular basis, often suffer from serious health problems as a result of the stress that is put on their bodies by their unnatural lifestyle. Sleep deprivation is another issue. Those who regularly work at night rarely catch up on missed sleep. Sleep deprivation is known to be a very effective form of torture. ...

Men in operational crews also lived in constant fear. Being part of an élite group did not immunise them against mental and physical break-down. Those who capitulated mentally would be summarily stood down and demoted or dismissed, and branded as LMF (lack of moral fibre), often by those who had never been put to the test in a similar way. Like the soldiers in the trenches in the First World War, they were sometimes 'lions led by donkeys'. Indeed, setting off on a dangerous bombing mission with the odds stacked against them must have felt much like 'going over the top'. Many, like my father, had had many close encounters with death by the end of their time in Bomber Command, even if they did survive in the end. And this took its toll.

Each of those who did manage to cope with the constant fear, which they all experienced, did so in his own way. Some worked hard and played hard, drinking and smoking excessively when not on duty, and generally sowing their wild oats, much as students often do, but for quite different reasons. They lived each day and night when they were not on a mission knowing that it could be their last, and this inevitably influenced their behaviour. Theirs was an existence of stark contrast, between life in a peaceful, rural backwater of England, and terrifying action over enemy territory. Some airmen were superstitious, and pinned their faith on talismans (like Dupueis, my father's flight engineer, with his not-so-lucky rabbit's foot). Some had 'lucky' garments (like Laurie Underwood's scarf) or rituals they performed before every op. Others were religious and relied on their faith to see them through.

They were all vulnerable, not just to the enemy, but also to their own potential fragility and to human error. Often, careless mistakes were made due to fatigue or complacency, if, for example, they were sent to lay mines or to bomb a 'safe' target.

However, some were meticulous in all that they did. My father has always been a careful and precise individual. I am not sure whether that is in his genetic make-up, or whether this aspect of his (sometimes obsessive) personality evolved as a reaction to the circumstances in which he found himself during the war. Before she died in 1986, my paternal grandmother once confided in me that my father had never been the same after the war, although she did not elaborate on this statement. I just know that he went away as a boy, not long after leaving school, and came back as a man who sometimes seemed to be carrying the weight of the whole world on his slim shoulders.

My father firmly believes that he saved his life by means of the parachute ritual and mantra he described so fully in his own notes. Ever since that time, he has lived his life with a metaphorical parachute strapped to his back. Crews often had collective rituals or practices. Johnny Bushell and my father undoubtedly owed their lives to ignoring official policy, by having their parachutes at the ready, and not stowed away in the designated storage space. This was a reaction to the narrow escape they had had on their first operation.

The camaraderie of crews had to develop very quickly, as the death rate meant that they sometimes needed to regroup. My father still talks with enormous affection of the other three members of his crew who survived being shot down. He believes that it is highly significant that they knew each other really well and socialised together when not on duty (although he knew Laurie and Johnny better than 'Griff', because the latter had only taken over the crew after they had lost their previous two pilots). These colleagues were his surrogate family. The four men relied on each other for moral support. Dad had a particularly close relationship with his rear gunner, Johnny Bushell, as the two of them not only survived the crash, but ended up as 'muckers' together for twelve months of their fifteen months of captivity. Dad was really troubled when Johnny finally passed away, leaving him as the 'last one standing'. He still asks himself why he should be the last one left. There is no answer to that question.

Teamwork and mutual support could sustain a crew and enable them to cope in the most challenging of circumstances. When crews were split up for any reason, and individuals had to regroup, it was sometimes necessary to fly as a 'spare' with a strange crew. This had happened to my father on a number of occasions, before he teamed up with his final crew. He hated flying as a spare, because it was the worst possible scenario. He disliked the additional lack of security of not knowing his fellow crewmembers, and found it hard to cope with the intense feelings of isolation that he then experienced during a mission. Cohesion was important for mental health, as well as for sheer existence. Surviving after a narrow escape together would not only strengthen a crew, it would also make them more methodical in their routines, and less likely to take unnecessary risks on subsequent trips, as my father's experiences have demonstrated.

There was no room for mavericks. There is, as they say, no 'I' in team. Crews had to pull together, and so did groups of crews who were flying in formation, engaged on the same mission. Lone aircraft were especially vulnerable to attack from night fighters. One had to stay in the bombing stream. Just as in the animal kingdom, there was safety in numbers. A stray bomber provided easy pickings once coned in a searchlight or identified by a fighter pilot. Once a bomber had been hit by a night fighter or by flak, but especially by the former, its crew only had a one in five chance of survival. In my father's crew, the survival rate was 50%, which defied these odds! Whether this was due to luck or judgement, we will never know. Dad thinks it was a bit of both.

Exhaustion was the result of constant stress, fear and anticipation. It also resulted from a lack of sleep, and sometimes from living it up too much between raids. Occasionally, adverse weather conditions or other operational difficulties grounded crews for days or even weeks at a time.

This was a mixed blessing, as long gaps between ops – although they allowed crews important 'down time' – meant that a tour would last longer. Some men were keen to do their thirty ops and then 'get the hell out'. They were entitled to stand down after one tour, although many individuals elected to do two or more.

Periods of inactivity also gave the crew time to reflect. I eventually summoned up the courage to ask my father (as did a German journalist) whether he had ever thought about the German civilians who were killed by the bombs dropped by his aircraft. Dad paused, and then said that he never had time to do this on a raid, as the job of a navigator was totally cerebral, and he was constantly occupied in keeping the plane on track, both on the way to the target and on the way home. He was also better able to focus on the task, and not give in to his fear, while he was sitting at his little table, as this was curtained off from the rest of the fuselage. He was his own man, as well as being pivotal to the safety of his crew. Other crewmembers, such as the gunners, had long periods of inactivity during ops, when their thoughts might wander. This could be dangerous, as it could lead to lapses in concentration and vigilance, although gunners were in constant visual contact with their surroundings, sitting for hours on end in their turrets.

Dad did confess that when grounded at Pocklington for any length of time, such as in early January 1944, he had plenty of time to reflect and to examine his conscience. His own writing shows us that he is a man of balance and compassion, who sees the shades of grey as well as the black and white issues. He did not enjoy bombing, although I believe that he gained a great deal of personal satisfaction from using his considerable navigational skills, which were officially recognised as being exceptional. Plotting his courses carefully clearly appealed to the perfectionism in his character. As far as his conscience was concerned, he reasoned that he simply had a job to do, and so he just did it to the very best of his ability. It was as simple as that. He was one of a team, which was part of Bomber Command, which played an important role in Britain's war offensive, which was in turn part of the Allied offensive against Nazism, which is how the Allied war was won. That is how he justified his actions. His remarks about individual Germans, both during the war and subsequently, show that his attitude is balanced and is in no way jingoistic or xenophobic. His criticisms of other Britons equally, show that he is a discerning judge of character, which overrides nationality. We do not choose our nationality, but we all make decisions about how we choose to live our lives.

On his first trip back to Berlin in 2001 with the Stalag IVB Association, dad made a specific request to the coach driver to include the Kaiser Wilhelm Memorial Church in Berlin on their tour. This is the church whose bombed-out remains have been retained, next to the ultra-modern replacement church, to serve as a reminder of the horror of war. The idea is similar to the one behind the rebuilt Coventry Cathedral. In 2001, there had been no time to do anything other than drive past the church in the coach. In October 2005, when I took my parents back to Berlin at the beginning of our quest for the crash site, dad once again asked that we make time for a visit to this church in our itinerary. Dad is not a religious man, so at the time I did not read anything into his request, as the church is a popular tourist attraction and is one of the most iconic landmarks in modern Berlin.

However, in 2005, my father sat for what seemed like hours in the Kaiser Wilhelm Church, motionless in the middle of a sea of blue light. Even on a dull day, one has the impression of being underwater when inside the church. The beautiful blue stained glass, inspired by that of the famous Chartres Cathedral in France, forms most of the enormous modern windows. These have an abstract design that gives one an intense feeling of tranquillity. Even the non-religious cannot fail to be touched by the church's intensely spiritual and mesmeric atmosphere. The redesigned church was conceived as a symbol of reconciliation between nations. It contains an iron cross from Russia, and a cross made of nails from the ruins of the original Coventry Cathedral, which was destroyed by German bombs in 1940. The rebuilt Kaiser Wilhelm Church was consecrated on the same day in May 1962 as the new Coventry Cathedral. This was a highly symbolic moment of international reconciliation. But in October 2005, dad was making his own private peace with the Berliners, sixty-two years after being involved in the raid that destroyed the original church.

While my father was sitting in the church, which I had already visited on a number of occasions, the first of which had been as a student in July 1979, I had a look round the various exhibits. One of these was a charcoal drawing of the Madonna and child, known as the Stalingrad Madonna. This had been sketched at Christmas 1942 on the back of a Russian map, by a German, Kurt Reuber. Kurt was a medical officer and pastor, serving on the Eastern Front. He died in captivity in a Russian prison camp on 20 January 1944, probably having suffered terribly at the hands of his Russian captors. This date was an amazing coincidence. Once again, it reminded me of the terrible suffering that is endured by all sides in all conflicts. For on the very same day on which my father had been shot down by a German night fighter in the skies over Berlin, and had lost four of his crewmembers, a German prisoner had perished in inhuman conditions in a Russian camp. These were two seemingly insignificant and unconnected events in the grand scheme of things. To me, they are a tragic and poignant snapshot of a much bigger picture.

I get the impression that during the war years, my father never shared his fear and anxiety with his own immediate family, even when he was on leave. He did not want to add to their anxiety by burdening them with his own. In the same way, they protected him from their own troubles in their letters to him. For example, when their family home was hit by an incendiary bomb, they did not tell him about it, as they felt that he had enough on his plate (metaphorically, if not literally), being a POW.

In November 2013, I asked my father whether he had ever shared his troubles with anyone else during the war years, in order to keep his sanity. He replied that he had received a lot of support from his former Boy's Brigade captain, Mr Heron, who had acted as a sounding board when my father was home on leave, as well as by writing to him. This was a new and interesting revelation, which proved that there are things I will never know about my father, no matter how many questions I may ask of him. In many ways, he is still a very private man, although far less so these days than formerly. Mr Heron wrote more letters to my father than any other person while he was in captivity. Dad was also to turn to him when he needed a bed for the night after arriving in London late one night, sometime after VE Day, in May 1945. So Mr Heron was the first person from 'home' to see my emaciated father after he returned from captivity.

Dad's feelings have been on a constant rollercoaster throughout his adult life.

In 1944, after being shot down, he was at first elated to be alive. He then experienced constant shifts of emotion (his own account demonstrates this) as his fortunes waxed and waned throughout his time in captivity.

During the immediate post-war years, he tried to live quietly with his troubling memories, without inflicting them on others. This seems to have been common among Second World War veterans. They were not encouraged to talk about their experiences, but just to have the proverbial 'stiff upper lip' and carry on. However, these memories occasionally rose to the surface from his subconscious mind, and caused him to have horrific nightmares, which continued well into the 1960s, as I recall. They may have carried on long after that. I have never asked him about this.

In 1994, when he finally met up again with the other three survivors, they all experienced joy and companionship – and even a little guilt, I suspect, that they had survived and that the four others hadn't.

In 2001, my father was amazed by the kind and compassionate treatment that he and other veterans received from German people, when he and my mother first visited Mühlberg am Elbe, and the site of the former Stalag IVB POW camp. Having been exposed for years to the jaundiced view of the German people held by many post-war Britons, dad was reassured that his own more balanced feelings about them had been reinforced by new experiences. One cannot overemphasise the danger of stereotyping people of any nationality, since there really are no 'norms'. Human beings are simply human.

My father was profoundly shocked and traumatised by the heart attack he suffered in May 2002. It was his fourth 'near miss', the other three having been in wartime. However, its legacy was positive in that it made him face up to his own mortality; it galvanised him into action, as subsequently he sat down and wrote up his wartime notes for posterity. Without them, this book would not have been written! I believe that the heart attack also intensified his resolve to take over where George Griffiths had left off, and find out more about what had really happened to his plane and to the rest of his crew on 20 January 1944.

In 2005, my father experienced once more the mixed emotions of a Stalag IVB reunion in Mühlberg am Elbe, followed by a second trip to Berlin, during which we were introduced to the eyewitness, Michael Pincus. This turning point, together with the enormous commitment of the people of Köpenick, enabled us to pursue our quest for the crash site.

This further strengthened my father's respect for German people.

The remnants of the plane were found in 2006 and, later, the human remains of John Bremner. Locating the plane wreckage was very exciting, but the discovery of John's remains unleashed a torrent of emotion with which my father really struggled. It resurrected the 'survivor's guilt', and brought back nightmare memories of his descent from 18,000 feet above Berlin, to eventual captivity.

He met Leopold Fellerer's grandson in 2007 but, happily, this was a wholly positive and cathartic experience, in the midst of the long period of frustration before the identity of the human remains was established.

In 2008 came the visits to Elvington and Pocklington, and the flight in the glider, during which he once more wore a parachute. This must have been a hair-raising experience for a man of eighty-five. Naturally, the most important event in that year was John Bremner's funeral. Like all funerals it was a sad occasion, but also an opportunity to celebrate John's short life and to marvel at what had been achieved between 2005 and 2008, leading up to the funeral. Dad was adamant that this was a collective achievement. He has never tried to take sole credit for it, or attempted to glorify it.

The year 2009 saw my father rewarded by the Royal Institute of Navigation (see below) for his part in discovering John Bremner's remains. This was indeed a proud moment. And the 2012 opening of the Bomber Command Memorial in Green Park, London, was also deeply satisfying, and long overdue.

During 2013, we marked my father's ninetieth birthday, and celebrated his longevity. This joy was tempered by the sadness associated with the loss of the other two surviving crewmembers, Laurie Underwood and Johnny Bushell. Because dad was 'the last man standing', that year our thoughts inevitably turned to those who were no longer with us. Apart from the recently deceased Johnny and Laurie, this included Griff, the pilot, Jackie, whose remains we buried in 2008, and Eric and Ken, whose graves were already in Berlin when we laid Jackie to rest there.

It is still a matter of great sadness that Charles Dupueis, dad's Canadian mid-upper gunner, remains unaccounted for. It would have been wonderful to have been able to close the chapter on his life as well, but we will just have to hope that his grave is, as we suspect, one of the unmarked ones in the row adjacent to that of Ken Stanbridge. Sadly, we will probably never know the truth.

My dad, Reg, has never been a very demonstrative man, but the extent to which he was deeply moved by Jacky Bremner's funeral and its aftermath was evident in the considerable national TV, radio and press coverage that ensued. He was interviewed by ITN and the BBC, as well as LBC radio. The story was covered thoroughly by BBC TV news, Radio Wales, Radio 3, Radio 4 (The *Today* programme and the *PM* programme), Radio 5 Live and, most extensively, by ITN news, who had filmed Reg at home, as well as interviewing him.

The German (Berlin) TV services also covered the event, as did numerous newspapers such as *Berliner Woche*, *Berliner Kurrier* and the prestigious *Berliner Morgenpost*. In the UK there was coverage in the *Daily Mail*, the *Daily Express*, *The Times* and the *Telegraph*, as well as a number of local and regional newspapers.

Such extensive exposure in the media might have made Reg into a celebrity, at least for a short time, but he did not let this happen. He claims to have been humbled by the experience, and yet, without his sustained efforts, we would never have found the wreckage of his bomber, or his comrade in arms.

Notwithstanding Reg's tenacity in seeing his dream fulfilled, it is important to stress that he was not acting in isolation. In spite of his strenuous efforts, none of these incredible events would have taken place without the commitment of the MoD and of our new German friends: journalists, curators, historians and eyewitnesses. Out of the misery of war and its aftermath, we built up a huge network of friends and contacts, both here in the UK and overseas. We had some wonderful moments together. This story reminds us of the unquestionable horror of war but, at the same time, it shows us how even the worst of conflicts can lead to deep and lasting national and international friendships.

News of Reg's quest to find the crash site of his plane, and the consequent discovery of his comrade's remains, somehow came to the attention of the Royal Institute of Navigation (RIN).

The RIN is a learned society with charitable status. It was formed in 1947, and is based in London. Its stated aims are: 'To unite all those with a professional or personal interest in any aspect of navigation in one unique body; to further the development of navigation in every sphere; and to increase public awareness of the art and science of navigation.'

In the spring of 2009, Reg received a letter from the RIN, in which he was invited to accept an award for his endeavours and their consequences for John Bremner's family. The award was presented to Reg by HRH Prince Philip, Duke of Edinburgh, in July of that year. This proved to be a very special and happy occasion, attended by my parents, myself and my two siblings, Robert and Helen. We have treasured photographs of the event but, to this day, we have no idea who nominated Reg for the award which he was truly honoured to receive.

Recognition for Bomber Command

It had long been a cause of sorrow and even anger among Bomber Command veterans that their part in bringing about the downfall of Hitler's Germany had never been properly recognised. The dashing young pilots of Fighter Command, who flew in their beloved Spitfires, and who brought about victory in the Battle of Britain, have often been fêted and celebrated. In contrast, the issue of the area bombing carried out by Bomber Command crews in the second half of the war became a red hot potato – even an embarrassment – particularly in the aftermath of the controversial bombing of Dresden in February 1945. It is somehow acceptable to glorify those who defended the realm, but not even to commend the courage of those who were involved in the bomber offensive.

Essential and legitimate bombing targets were deemed to be those whose destruction might bring about a degree of hindrance to or devastation of the enemy's war machine, although this definition was far from precise. Did it, for example, include the demoralisation of the enemy? And how, exactly, was this to be achieved? In the early years of Bomber Command, only specific strategic targets were attacked, although it was always accepted that collateral damage was an inevitable (if undesirable) consequence of any aerial attack, especially in the days when navigational technology was in its infancy. True and accurate precision bombing was a long time coming, because of the rudimentary navigation techniques that were still being used in the early stages of the war. However, from 1943 onwards, in spite of the considerable advances made in navigational and bomb-aiming technology, area bombing became the norm. This was partly due to a polemic conviction held by Arthur (Bomber) Harris, that this was the only way to hasten the end of the conflict in Europe. Area bombing attacks were to continue even after D-Day and the securing of the Second Front, right up until the final days of the war in the spring of 1945. The inevitable consequences of this were huge numbers of civilian casualties and considerable damage to non-strategic targets.

Even in the midst of the Allies' fierce and courageous battle against the Nazi war machine, area bombing had its critics in Britain. And after the war, when the scale and immediacy of the Nazi threat to the British way of life had been forgotten, Churchill and his successors were to quietly turn their backs on Bomber Command veterans, as to honour them would have meant risking political suicide. To be seen to do this was never going to be a vote winner, and from the end of March 1945 onwards, Churchill soon evolved from a wartime leader into a peacetime politician, who was quick to distance himself from the whole messy business of dropping bombs on German people, even if this had initially been in response to the London Blitz. This attitude of denial has prevailed among the vast majority of post-war politicians.

Bomber Command veterans campaigned in vain for more than six decades for public recognition of their part in the war effort, and of the huge personal sacrifices that were made. There is no doubt that the intensive bombing of Germany, especially in 1943 and 1944, hastened the end of the conflict by many months, if not longer.

It would not be appropriate for me to go into any great detail here about the long and ultimately successful campaign to honour the fallen heroes of Bomber Command with a national memorial, as this story has been competently covered elsewhere. Suffice it to say that the memorial was financed by years of dedicated fundraising by enthusiasts. Once again, appeals to Government to show its support for the Bomber Command Memorial appeal, and for the idea of awarding these veterans a proper campaign medal, fell on profoundly deaf ears. Needless to say, Reg was present at the unveiling of the Bomber Command Memorial in Green Park by the Queen on 28 June 2012. The event was not even shown on live television in the UK, such is the reluctance, even today, of mealy-mouthed politicians to honour the 55,573 forgotten heroes of Bomber Command. But we will remember them. ...

In February 2013, one month after Reg's ninetieth birthday, it was announced that eligible veterans of Bomber Command would finally be awarded with a 'clasp' to wear on their 1939–45 Stars. Many veterans expressed their dismay that they would only receive a clasp, and not a proper, if very belated, campaign medal for their service. After the war, a disgusted Arthur Harris had expressed his anger that the brave aircrews of Bomber Command were not honoured in this way. Reg received his clasp in the late summer of 2013. His rear gunner, Johnny Bushell, received his in June 2013, the day before he died. Many of the applications for these clasps have been made by the relatives of veterans who have passed away in the years that have elapsed while their struggle for recognition has been continuing. Similarly, many veterans did not live to see the unveiling of the Bomber Command Memorial in 2012.

On 20 January 2014, Reg Wilson commemorated the seventieth anniversary of his leap of faith into the treacherous skies over Berlin. Six days later, he celebrated his ninety-first birthday, shortly followed by the sixtieth anniversary of his marriage to Barbara, my mother, on 20 March 2014. He is the last-surviving member of the crew of Halifax LW337, since both Laurie Underwood and Johnny Bushell sadly passed away in 2013, Laurie on 20 February and Johnny on 16 June.

A tribute to Bomber Command crews by Noel Coward:

LIE IN THE DARK AND LISTEN

Lie in the dark and listen,
It's clear tonight so they're flying high
Hundreds of them, thousands perhaps,
Riding the icy, moonlit sky.
Men, machinery, bombs and maps
Altimeters and guns and charts
Coffee, sandwiches, fleece-lined boots
Bones and muscles and minds and hearts,
English saplings with English roots
Deep in the earth they've left below.
Lie in the dark and let them go;

Lie in the dark and listen.

Lie in the dark and listen.
They're going over in waves and waves
High above villages, hills and streams,
Country churches and little graves
And little citizens' worried dreams.
Very soon they'll have reached the sea
And far below them will lie the bays
And cliffs and sands where they used to be
Taken for summer holidays.
Lie in the dark and let them go;
Theirs is a world you'll never know
Lie in the dark and listen.

Lie in the dark and listen.
City magnates and steel contractors,
Factory workers and politicians
Soft hysterical little actors, ballet dancers,
'reserved' musicians,
Safe in your warm civilian beds,
Count your profits and count your sheep
Life is passing above your heads
Just turn over and try to sleep.
Lie in the dark and let them go
There's one debt you'll forever owe,
Lie in the dark and listen.

Regarding Reginald Wilson (13 May 2009)

I understand that Mr Eric Buesnel has proposed that Reg Wilson be nominated for the possible award of an MBE and I am writing in support of that proposal.

Halifax LW337 was shot down over Berlin during an operation on the night of the 20th January 1944. Of the eight man crew, four successfully baled out to safety, and the remaining four lost their lives. Two of the missing crew were never recovered. The four survivors included my late father, George Griffiths DFM, who was the pilot, and Reg Wilson, the navigator.

I understand that not knowing where that aircraft had eventually crashed nor the fate of the two missing crew members had troubled Reg down the years, and in 2005 he determined to find it. Some time before he died in 1998 my father had sent Reg a map with a rough indication of where he thought the aircraft may have come down in woodland on the outskirts of Berlin. With the help of this small clue Reg set about locating the wreckage, aided by his daughter Janet, a fluent German speaker. He enlisted the help of the German Press and a local appeal led to the discovery of a surviving eye witness which narrowed the search. Combing the woodland with metal detectors produced a numbered fragment of wreckage which enabled him to establish the crash site conclusively. To his shock, excavation of the site recovered human remains which DNA testing proved to be those of Sgt. Jackie Bremner, one of the missing crew.

In October 2008 my mother, Hazel Griffiths, and I attended the funeral of Sgt. Jackie Bremner at the War Cemetery in Berlin. He was buried with full military honours 64 years after his death with his elder sister, Marjorie Acon, in attendance.

It was a privilege to be there, and an incredibly moving experience. It brought home to me on such a personal level the great sacrifice these incredibly young men had made. Standing amongst the rows and rows of fallen airmen, it was hard to imagine the courage it must have taken for them to go out on operations night after night, when so many of their friends failed to return and knowing that their own odds for survival in Bomber Command were slight.

I know that the funeral brought closure to the families, most particularly to the Bremner family. Poignantly, the son of wireless operator Eric Church and the daughter of second pilot Kenneth Stanbridge, both born after the deaths of their fathers, were traced and were able to visit their fathers' graves for the first time.

Although Reg's story can be summarised into one neat paragraph, it fails in every way to convey the enormity of his task. His persistence, perseverance and tenacity enabled him to accomplish this and the cooperation of the German people was heart-warming. His work also brought wide media coverage, raising awareness again of the sacrifice, courage and heroism of those people who died so young with their lives unfulfilled. I think it is important that we never forget them.

Karen Griffiths, 2 June 2009

Acknowledgements

As I have stressed many times throughout the course of this book, Reg's success in making his remarkable discovery could not have been achieved without the contributions of the following people, to whom we will be eternally grateful. Without their efforts, finding the Halifax aircraft would not have happened and this book would never have been written. We would like to thank the following people, whose names have been listed in the order in which they became involved in the project:

- The late George Griffiths, Reg's pilot, whose initial research and procurement of the map of the approximate crash site led directly to the subsequent quest and discovery.

- The RAF Museum, Hendon, and the Public Records Office, Kew.

- The Commonwealth War Graves Commission.

- The late Claus-Dieter Sprink, curator of the Köpenick Heimatmuseum, whose enthusiasm for our project enabled us to continue our research in Berlin. Sadly, Claus-Dieter did not live to see the huge impact of his early involvement, as he died in 2006.

- Ralf Drescher, freelance journalist. Ralf has been absolutely pivotal to the success of this project. His initial article in the local newspaper, *Berliner Woche*, enabled us to sift through the accounts of numerous contemporary eyewitnesses, until we made the critical breakthrough. Ralf's interest in the project has continued since our first contact with him in the autumn of 2005, and is ongoing. He has become a close family friend. We thank him for his kind permission to use his photographs.

- Michael Pincus, retired Berlin dentist. Michael proved to be the critical eyewitness whose schoolboy sketch of January 1944 forms the cover of this book. The information he provided was absolutely crucial to our later discovery.

- Rüdiger Kaddatz of www.luftkrieg-oberhavel.de – Rüdi's input, and local knowledge, together with his metal detector, enabled us to achieve the final breakthrough. His account of the events (in German) can be found on his website.

- Stefan Salem, grandson of Hauptmann Fellerer, for his friendship and insight.

- The MoD and, in particular, Sue Raftree of the JCCC, for her commitment and organisation of events, most especially in the critical year of 2008.

- Paul and Lesley Fallon, close relatives of the late John Bremner, whose constructive suggestions during the latter stages of writing this book have been invaluable. Their personal insight into the loss of John Bremner and its impact on their family has been most poignant.

- The BBC and ITN for their sensitive and thorough media coverage of the events in October 2008.

- Steve Darlow, my publisher, for believing in me and for considering this story to be worthy of publication.

Last, but not least, I should like to thank my family for their support and encouragement. Firstly, to my mother, Barbara Wilson, who kept insisting that I should write this book, and made me finally get down to doing it! Before dad's original handwritten notes were usable, my mother's typing and proofreading skills were invaluable in the period leading up to 2005, when dad finally completed his notes and circulated them to family members so that his story would be recorded for posterity. Dad's notes form the core of the book. My own immediate family have been long-suffering and supportive while I have been writing and redrafting this book. My thanks go to my husband David, and our children, Katherine and Christopher, together with my brother Robert, my sister Helen and their respective families. Together, we are providing continuing support to Reg, our father, grandpa, and family hero, and to our beloved mother and gran.

Bibliography and Sources

Information about the London bombing of 29 December 1940:
http://en.wikipedia.org/wiki/Second_Great_Fire_of_London

Information about Oflag VIIB, Eichstätt, Bavaria, and the 'friendly fire'
incident: *http://www.geocities.ws/pda295/pow/index.htm*

Propaganda clip about Hauptmann Fellerer:
https://www.youtube.com/watch?v=FCzTzenwlil

Commonwealth War Graves Commission website: *http://www.cwgc.org*

Yorkshire Air Museum website:
http://www.yorkshireairmuseum.org/exhibits/aircraft-exhibits/world-war-two-aircraft/handley-page-halifax-iii

Gibb, R., Dooley, J., Darlow, S., Feast, S. and Rayner, G. *The Bomber
Command Memorial* (Fighting High, 2012)

Hastings, M., *Bomber Command* (Pan Military Classics, 1979, Kindle
edition)

Index

Squadrons/ Groups

Y

Z